Creative Miniature Quilts

Kerry Gadd

Creative HOUSE

First published in 2002 by
Creative House
(an imprint of Sally Milner Publishing Pty Ltd)
PO Box 2104
Bowral NSW 2576
AUSTRALIA

© Kerry Gadd 2002

Design and illustrations by Anna Warren, Warren Ventures Pty Ltd
Editing by Anne Savage
Photography by Sergio Santos

Printed in China by Leefung-Asco Printers Ltd

National Library of Australia Cataloguing-in-Publication data:

Gadd, Kerry, 1950- .
    Creative miniature quilts.

    ISBN 1 877080 01 2.

    1. Miniature quilts. 2. Patchwork - Patterns. I. Title.

    746.46041

10 9 8 7 6 5 4 3 2 1

Contents

Projects (in order of difficulty)

Introduction

MY FIRST QUILT was a traditional pattern made from instructions given in a magazine. Up until then my sewing expertise lay in making soft toys, dolls' clothes and clothing for my family. Making a quilt should have been easy. Wrong! I decided that if I was going to continue I had better learn how to do it properly and took a class in the basics—and I recommend this to anyone who is just beginning.

Now thoroughly bitten by the quilting bug, I found so many designs that I wanted to make, but there never seemed to be enough time. It was at this point that I turned from making full size quilts to making miniatures to satisfy my enthusiasm. That was sixteen years ago and I am just as committed to making them now as I was then.

Whenever I see a quilt design that I like or an interesting block, I wonder what it would look like in miniature. Although I now use the computer for designing, I still draft the blocks onto graph paper, scaling them down and changing them if necessary for easier piecing.

Miniatures are a great way to try out different block and quilt designs that could eventually be made into a larger quilt; they are also a great way to audition fabric combinations and use up those precious scraps. They do not use a lot of fabric so they are not expensive to make, and can be finished in a couple of days.

Sometimes people are nervous of making miniatures because of the size of the pieces—or rather, their lack of size. I tell my students that they are not actually handling small pieces all the time; really, they are just sewing larger pieces that will be cut down to size.

Miniature quilt making is fun and if you remember the three Ps—Patience, Practice and Perseverance—before long you will have a gallery of wonderful little miniature quilts. The most important thing to remember, if you are just beginning, is not to expect your first quilt to be perfect! Miniature quilt making is like anything else—practice makes perfect. With any luck you will become as addicted to making miniature quilts as I am.

I have been teaching miniature quilt making for the last twelve years, and my students have long wanted to know when I was going to write a book about miniatures or supply them with patterns. To all my students past and future—here it is.

Fabric and equipment

Fabric

IN SELECTING FABRICS for miniatures, try to keep the weight of the fabrics the same. The most satisfactory fabrics are 100 per cent cottons—they press cleanly and the seams don't 'pop' open as they do with polyester. If a light fabric is sewn to a heavier one, the lighter fabric tends to distort, making small block units very hard to handle and keep square. Lightweight fabrics are hard to use, as they tend to fray easily, so avoid them where possible.

Wash and press all fabric before use to remove sizing and to check on colourfastness. If, after repeated washings, the dye in a particular fabric still runs, get rid of it. It is also easier to press the fabric while still damp. Always check on fabric widths when buying, especially if buying for borders. In fact, sometimes I will make the quilt top and then go shopping for the border fabric. I always buy an extra 4 inches (10 cm) more than given requirements if I am making a quilt from a purchased pattern. Because of this, amounts given for the projects are generous and are all based on 44 inch (112 cm) wide fabric. I would rather have fabric left over than be short. It's good for the stash as well. Fat quarters and charm squares are excellent for miniature quilt making. A fat quarter is an 18 inch (50 cm) length of fabric that is cut down the middle, on the lengthwise grain, yielding two identical pieces of fabric measuring 18 x 22½ inches (50 x 56 cm). Charm squares are samples of fabric ranging from 6 to 8 inches (15 to 20 cm) square, the size depending on the retailer's preference.

Colour choice is very important. Choose fabrics that contrast well with each other. Complementary or analogous colours are better choices than monochromatic. If there is not enough contrast between them, the pieces tend to 'bleed' or blend into each other visually, and there is nothing more disheartening than to lose all those tiny points you worked so hard to achieve.

If you have trouble in selecting fabrics, try this method. Select a fabric that you really like. Study the colours within it. This will give you several possible colourways you could work with. By auditioning fabrics like this you can sometimes come up with surprising combinations.

The background fabric is very important. It must be neutral so the small pieces within the blocks stand out. In most of my miniatures I use white, cream, or white on white, etc. Dark background fabrics can look great but remember that the other fabrics used must have a high degree of contrast.

Fabrics with large areas of background in a neutral colour do not work well for block piecing, especially if the background fabric of the block is neutral as well. However, they work really well in the borders.

Grain line

Fabrics suitable for quilting have three different grain lines—crosswise, lengthwise and bias—as shown in figure 1.

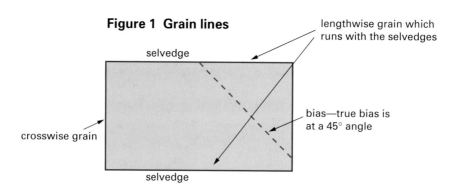

Figure 1 Grain lines

lengthwise grain which runs with the selvedges

selvedge

bias—true bias is at a 45° angle

crosswise grain

selvedge

The lengthwise grain is the strongest. There is little or no give when pulled. The crosswise grain has a slight amount of give and the bias grain has the most stretch.

The lengthwise and crosswise grain are often referred to as the 'straight' grain. When you are required to cut something on the straight grain, it must be either lengthwise or crosswise. When cutting squares, rectangles and strips they must be cut on the straight grain unless you are going to be doing bias strip piecing.

Thread

I like to use a neutral colour for the piecing. Beige, cream or light grey work well. When attaching borders and binding I match the thread to the fabric where possible. Use either 100 per cent cotton or a poly/cotton twist. When I machine quilt, I use the same thread used for the piecing, matching thread to fabric when required.

Batting

Avoid high lofted batting. Your quilt will end up lumpy, and it would be very hard to quilt. A thin batting works best for miniatures. I prefer pellon or polyester/cotton, as they are thick enough to show up quilting and thin enough to drape if required. If you want to achieve an antique look use a 100 per cent cotton batting, because it will shrink slightly when washed.

Sewing machine

Your sewing machine is your best friend. It must be in good working order. Clean frequently and put in a new needle regularly. A blunt needle pulls fabric, splits fibres and can cause uneven seam allowances.

If possible, try to have a ¼ inch foot that fits your machine. I consider this to be essential rather than desirable. (For those of you working in metric, I have found that using the number 1 Bernina foot and running the fabric along the edge of it will result in a seam 0.75 cm wide.) Keep the stitch length at 13 stitches per inch (10 stitches per 2 cm). If I have to unpick a seam, the stitches are easy to remove and there is less wear on the fabric.

Rotary cutters

There are many types of rotary cutter on the market so shop around to find the one that suits you and your particular needs. Be careful, as they are dangerous. Keep away from children. Get into the habit of engaging the safety shield every time you have finished cutting and before you put the cutter down. Be especially careful in workshop situations. Make sure there are no pins around when cutting, as cutting over a pin will kill a blade instantly.

Keep a spare blade handy and use the old ones for cutting paper. Make sure they are stored away safely or disposed of properly.

Rotary cutting mats

Always use a proper rotary cutting mat or the cutter blade will be damaged, not to mention the surface you cut on. Never leave the mat in the sun and always store it flat. The best size is 17 x 23 inches (43 x 60 cm). It will accommodate fabric folded selvedge to selvedge. Anything smaller can be a handicap. Just because you are making a miniature quilt doesn't mean your mat has to be mini too!

Rulers

There is a wide range of sizes and brands of ruler made specifically for rotary cutting. Ordinary plastic rulers are no good, as the rotary cutter blade takes chunks out of them—and usually out of your fingers as well. The ruler you use must have ⅛ inch (0.25 cm) markings. This is essential when making miniatures, as the majority of cutting instructions use ⅛ inch (0.25 cm) increments.

I use three different rulers—a 6½ x 12½ inch (15 x 32 cm) ruler for smaller pieces of fabric; a much longer one, 6½ x 24 inches (15 x 60 cm), for cutting strips off fabric bulk-folded selvedge to selvedge, and a bias square ruler. The bias square ruler is essential for precise construction of the bias squares that are found in nearly all quilt blocks. This ruler is 6½ inches (20 cm) square and has ⅛ inch (0.25 cm) markings and a 45° line marked on the diagonal, corner to corner. It is one of the most important tools used in miniature quilt making.

There are many other rulers designed for specific purposes, but the three listed above are all you need to construct the quilts in this book. If possible, work with rulers of the same brand, as some brands are not compatible with each other. Always check compatibility before cutting anything.

Extra tools

Quick unpicker This is used not only to remove mistakes but as an extra finger. Use it to hold pieces of fabric together as they are fed under the foot of the machine. An awl would do the same job or a thin bamboo stick.

Scissors A small pair of very sharp scissors for snipping off threads and trimming down seam allowances.

Pins Long quilter's pins for pin basting.

Tape measure Marked in ⅛ inch and/or millimetre divisions.

Plastic bags Because there are lots of small scraps, a plastic bag taped to the worktable beside the machine stops some of the mess. It is also a good idea to have another one fairly handy to the cutting area.

Pin-up board A pin-up area to place finished blocks is essential. A board covered in flannel or batting, set up beside the machine, is handy and is the best way to organise the finished blocks. There is less chance of them being disturbed or lost and they are kept together if you need the project to be portable.

Key to diagrams

ruler

rotary cutter

– – – – – – – – – – stitching line

·························· cutting line

The insurance policy

I ENDOW ALL of my miniature quilts, during the cutting process, with insurance policies. There is nothing more frustrating than ending up with block units that are too small or won't fit together properly and thus with a miniature block that is distorted and uneven. The process I wish to share with you while you make the quilt projects is easy. It involves slightly more cutting than is normal with rotary cutting techniques, but the accuracy achieved in the finished product is worth the little extra effort. I work on the theory that a block unit can be cut down to the required size, because once cut, you cannot stick the pieces back on if you cut incorrectly. The extra time and attention and care taken with the extra cutting and pressing go towards making your miniature quilt as perfect as possible.

There is no denying that miniatures can become little monsters when they feel like it. There is no forgiveness and definitely no fudge factor. Accuracy is paramount, in cutting, sewing and even in pressing. Sometimes, no matter how careful you are in the cutting and sewing, the units that go together to form a block can end up either too small or crooked.

I overcome this risk by adding an 'insurance policy' to certain cutting stages. This method involves adding an extra ⅛ inch (0.25 cm), or more, to seam allowances when cutting some shapes and strips. These are then trimmed down to the exact required size after sewing and pressing. By doing this I know that all the particular units within a block are the exact size and the block then goes together perfectly. This method is also extremely handy when attaching narrow sashing strips and inner borders.

All cutting instructions for the quilt projects include ¼ inch (0.75 cm) seam allowances, and in some instances the instructions specify the extra ⅛ inch (0.25 cm) or more. However, some pieces must be cut the correct size. **Even though a cutting measurement might not sound correct, please do not alter it. Metric cutting sizes are not exact conversions; this is because an 0.75 cm**

seam allowance is larger than ¼ inch, so some of the insurance cuts for metric instructions are larger. All block divisions for the projects are ½ inch (1.25 cm) in finished size, except for Nautical Cats, where the divisions are ¾ inch (2 cm).

Preparing a straight edge

BEFORE CUTTING STRIPS from a piece of fabric, it is essential that the cut edges be trimmed straight. When preparing to cut strips, fold the fabric in half, selvedge to selvedge, with the fold closest to you. Place it on the cutting mat. Have the bulk of the fabric extending on your left-hand side. (If you are left-handed, reverse the instructions for this and for cutting, below.)

Using the long rotary ruler, place one of the lower horizontal lines on the fold of the fabric with the long vertical edge of the ruler as close to the raw edges as possible. Cut away the raw edges, leaving a straight clean edge, as shown in figure 2.

Figure 2 Preparing a straight edge

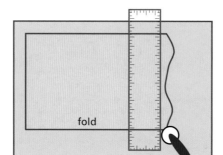

When cutting using the long ruler there is a tendency to hold the ruler firmly and make one cut. This action usually ends up with the top end of the ruler moving away. To stop this happening, begin with your left hand about a quarter of the way up the ruler. Cut until about level with your hand, then walk your fingers up the ruler. Cut again and walk your fingers again. This way your hand will always be slightly ahead of the cutting action.

Don't press or push too hard when cutting. If the blade is in good condition it will cut easily.

Cutting

Strips

AFTER PREPARING A straight edge, do not disturb the fabric, but turn the whole cutting mat around so the bulk of the fabric is now on the right-hand side. Line the ruler up again, this time with the horizontal line on the fold at the top and with the required measurement line on the straight cut edge. Make sure this line is actually on the fabric rather than just off it. I make sure there are a few threads extending beyond the required measurement line on the ruler. Quite often these few threads can make the difference in the finished size of the piece. See figure 3.

Figure 3 Cutting strips

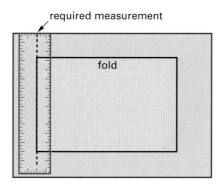

Strip-pieced units

It is easier to control long strip-pieced units by cutting the strips in half first, so you are only handling a 22 inch (56 cm) length at one time instead of a piece up to 44 inches (112 cm) long.

When sewing narrow strips together to form strip units, quite often you will find that the edges of the strips have developed a few bends or become distorted during pressing, especially if the seams are pressed in one direction, not open.

For all projects the strips for these units have had an extra ⅛ inch (0.25 cm) added. Sew together as instructed and press the seams open. The excess is then trimmed away leaving straight edges and a strip unit that is the exact width required for the project.

To do this, line up the ruler with the given measurement exactly on the seam line. Trim away the excess extending beyond the edge of the ruler on the right-hand side. Turn the unit around and repeat for the other side. This time you have two measurements to work with. Line up the required measurement exactly on the seam line again, with the remaining excess on the right. The left-hand edge of the unit will be in line with the required width of the strip unit. See figure 4.

**Figure 4 Cutting away excess fabric
from a strip pieced unit**

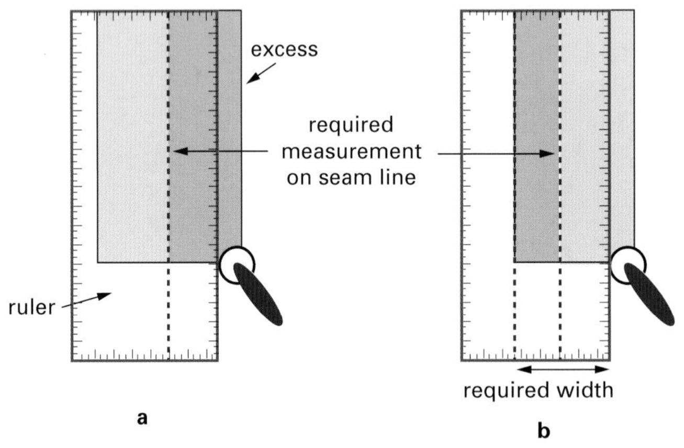

When cutting segments from strip-pieced units, one end needs to be squared up. To do this, align one of the horizontal lines of the ruler on a stitching line rather than an outside edge. Have the ruler as close as possible to the right-hand edge of the unit and trim. Turn the unit around and cut the required segments. Keep checking that the segments are straight. After cutting two or three away from the strip unit, you may have to square up the edge again, especially if the unit has a slight bend. This is normal and is a good practice to get into. With miniatures, the slightest inaccuracy can end up in a pieced unit not being square.

Sashing strips and inner border strips

Not only are narrow strips difficult to handle, they are nearly always distorted after pressing. To avoid this happening, some sashing strips and all inner borders have an extra ⅛ inch (0.25 cm) added to their width. The excess is trimmed away after sewing and pressing, leaving a straight even edge.

This extra only applies to sashing strips that have no posts, in other words unpieced vertical or horizontal long sashing strips.

Squares and rectangles

These are cut ½ inch (1.5 cm) larger than the required finished size. If 1 inch (2.5 cm) squares (finished size) are required, cut a strip 1½ inches (4 cm) wide and then cut into 1½ inch (4 cm) squares, as shown in figure 5.

Figure 5 Cutting squares

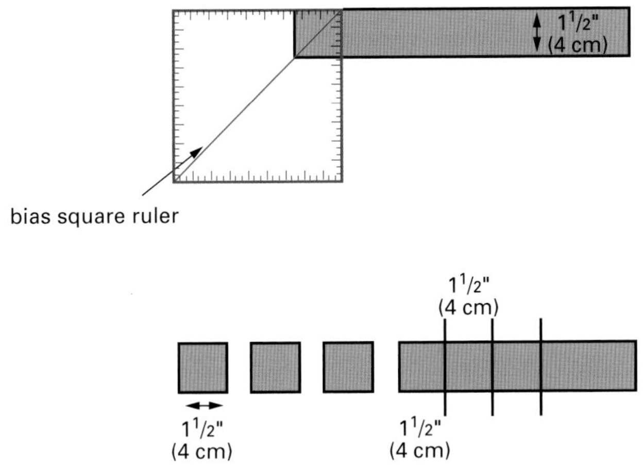

bias square ruler

If ½ x 1 inch (1.25 x 2.5 cm) rectangles (finished size) are required, cut a strip 1 inch (2.75 cm) wide, then cut into 1½ inch (4 cm) rectangles, as shown in figure 6. Sometimes it is more economical to cut the strips 1½ inches (4 cm) wide and then cut into 1 inch (2.75 cm) rectangles.

Figure 6 Cutting rectangles

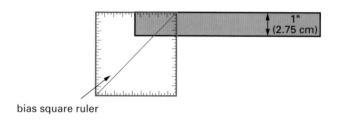

bias square ruler

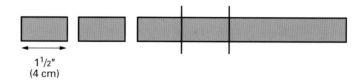

1¹/₂"
(4 cm)

Triangles

Half-square triangles

These are formed by cutting a parent square in half, diagonally once, to yield two triangles. The straight grain is on the two short legs, with the bias on the long diagonal leg. See figure 7.

Figure 7 Half-square triangles

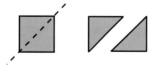

For standard rotary cutting, the parent square is cut ⅞ inch (2.5 cm) larger than the finished size of the short legs of the triangle. Unless I am making bias squares from these triangles (see page 19), I seldom alter this measurement.

When cutting squares from strips that are to be cut into half-square triangles from one fabric, double the strip and cut a pair of squares. Move the bulk of the strip away slightly and cut the squares diagonally once. Place the resulting triangles to one side and then cut another pair off the strip. If it is difficult to work out the right and wrong sides of the fabric, cut the strips in half and layer them right side to wrong side. This way the resulting triangles are all facing in the same direction, right or wrong sides up.

Quarter-square triangles

These are formed by cutting a parent square diagonally, twice, to yield four triangles. When cutting these diagonally, do not move the pieces until both diagonal cuts have been made. For standard rotary cutting, the parent square is cut 1¼ inch (3.5 cm) larger than the finished size of the long leg of the triangle. Because of the seam allowances involved I do not alter this measurement at all, unless I am cutting for the side-setting triangles. See figure 8.

Figure 8 Quarter-square triangles

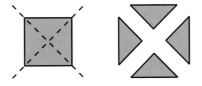

Bias squares

Bias squares are comprised of two half-square triangles sewn together on the bias edges. The quilt projects in this book use two different methods for constructing these.

Method 1: Bias squares made from half-square triangles

This method uses parent squares cut diagonally once to yield half-square triangles. The triangles are sewn together and the seam pressed open to form a bias square. Less fabric is required when using this method and it is an ideal way for constructing bias squares for scrap quilts.

The parent squares are cut 1 inch (3.25 cm) larger than the finished size of the bias squares. After the half-square triangles have been sewn together and the seam pressed open, the resulting square is too big. Using the bias square ruler, the excess is trimmed away leaving a bias square that is the exact size needed. Quite often the edges only need to be straightened slightly.

Example To make 1 inch (2.75 cm) bias squares, ½ inch (1.25 cm) finished size, cut two contrasting 1½ inch (4.5 cm) squares. Layer them right sides together and cut diagonally once. Sew the triangle pairs together. Press the seams open.

Use the bias square ruler to trim them down to 1 inch (2.75 cm). Align the 45° diagonal line on the bias square on the seam line. Leave a small amount of the square extending at the top and on the right-hand side. Trim these two edges. Rotate the square 180°. Position the trimmed edges where the two 1 inch (2.75 cm) lines on the ruler form a right angle and position the diagonal line on the stitching line again. Trim the remaining two sides. See figure 9.

Figure 9 Bias squares from half squares

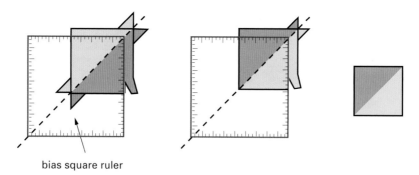

bias square ruler

If a project has bias squares made from two fabrics only, layer the two required fabric strips right sides together, cut a pair of squares and cut diagonally to form pairs of triangles that will be ready for sewing together. Repeat for the remaining strips.

Method 2: Bias strip units

This method is used to produce quick pieced bias squares.

Strips are cut on the bias grain of the fabric and sewn together along both long edges. These units are then cut into triangles that are pressed open to form bias squares. I find this method very accurate and you don't have all those little waste triangles lying around.

When cutting bias strips, position the ruler with the 45° diagonal line along the left-hand side of the fabric, with the edge of the ruler going through the top left-hand corner, as shown in figure 10a. Cut the required number of bias strips across the bulk of the fabric.

Figure 10 Cutting bias strips

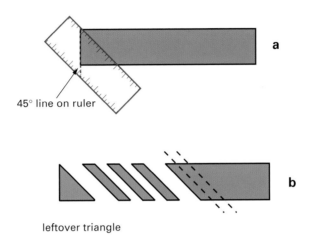

The leftover triangles from the corners can be used to cut into extra bias strips if required, or into squares and rectangles.

Strips are cut the width of the unfinished bias square. I add an extra ⅛ inch (0.5 cm) to this measurement.

Example To make 1 inch (2.75 cm) bias squares (½ inch (1.25 cm) finished size), cut two bias strips 1⅛ inch (3.25 cm) wide. Sew them together along both long edges. Press gently.

Lay the bias strip unit on the cutting mat. Locate where the two 1 inch (2.75 cm) marks lie on the edges of the bias square ruler. Place the ruler over the strip unit, with these two marks on the bottom stitching line and the left side of the ruler about ⅛ inch (0.5 cm) in from the left-hand edge. See figure 11a. Cut along the right-hand side of the ruler only, cutting away a triangle. See figure 11b.

Figure 11 Making bias squares

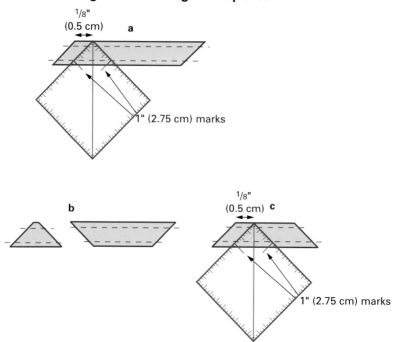

Flip the unit over, line up the 1 inch (2.75 cm) marks again and, leaving ⅛ inch (0.5 cm) on the left-hand edge, cut away another triangle. See figure 11c. Repeat flipping and cutting until the strip unit has been cut into triangles. The ⅛ inch (0.5 cm) remaining on the left-hand edge each time you cut is your insurance just in case the square moves when cutting, or the diagonal line was not exactly on the seam line for the first two cuts.

Remove the few stitches from the top of the triangle and press the seam open. If you put your finger between the two triangles and give a little tug, the stitching should pop apart. Use the bias square ruler to trim the square down to form a 1 inch (2.75 cm) bias square. Refer to page 20.

When cutting the strips for this method, one of the fabrics must be right side facing up and the other must have the right side facing down. To avoid confusion when cutting bias strips from background fabric, I always cut with the right side facing up. All other fabrics are cut right side facing down. If you are using only two fabrics to construct the bias squares, layer the two required fabrics right sides together, press, and then cut. The strips will be in pairs ready for sewing. This lessens the amount of handling on bias edges.

For some of the projects you will be instructed to cut bias strips from a single fabric layer. Be sure to have the fabric right side or wrong side up as instructed.

Pieced triangle units

Figure 12 Pieced triangle units

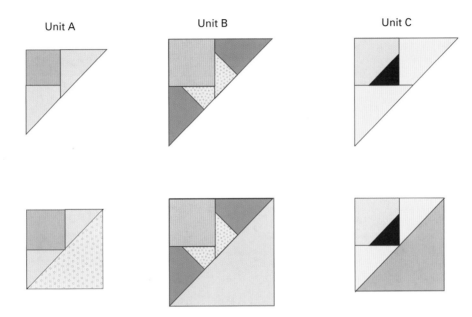

These units are formed when two half-square triangles are sewn to two sides of a square, as in unit A in figure 12; when two mirror-image units are sewn to a square, as in unit B, and when two half-square triangles are sewn to a bias square, as in unit C. Be careful when sewing the triangles to the square. The two edges of the triangle must be parallel with the two edges of the square or the bias edges of the finished unit will not be straight, as demonstrated in figure 13. Seam allowance accuracy is very important here.

Figure 13 Edges must be parallel or the unit will look like this

The resulting long sides of all pieced triangle units are on the bias grain. These units are normally sewn to a half-square triangle to form a square. Because of the bias edges involved, the pieced triangle unit can frequently distort, especially with small pieces. To avoid such disasters, I sew the pieced triangle unit to a square, as shown in figure 14, which is cut 1¼ inches (3.75 cm) larger than the finished width of the triangle unit.

Figure 14 Sewing the triangle unit to a square

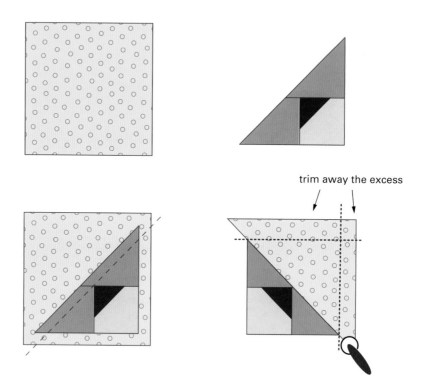

trim away the excess

After sewing and pressing the resulting unit is trimmed down, using the bias square ruler, to the required size, as shown in figure 14. The excess is removed from the back of the square to leave a ¼ inch (0.75 cm) seam allowance. This is done in the same manner as the as the last two cuts when cutting bias squares down to size (refer to figure 10). The base of the pieced triangle section rests in the right angle formed where the required measurement lines on the bias square come together on the diagonal line.

Sewing

UNLESS INDICATED OTHERWISE, a ¼ inch (0.75 cm) seam allowance is used for all projects. An accurate ¼ inch (0.75 cm) seam allowance is very important and I recommend that you practice the sewing test illustrated in figure 15 to develop accuracy.

Join three 1 x 3 inch (2.75 x 7.5 cm) strips together along the long edges. Press each seam open after sewing. If using a ¼ inch seam, the edges of the seam allowances should meet in the middle of the centre strip and the finished width of the centre strip will be ½ inch. If using an 0.75 cm seam, the centre strip will measure 1.25 cm and the edges of the seam allowances will overlap. These will need to be trimmed down to 0.5 cm to get rid of the extra bulk. (This will occur frequently in block and quilt assembly instructions when you are working in metric measurements, so please be aware of it.)

Figure 15 Sewing test

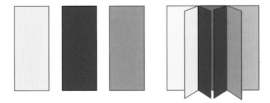

When sewing, do not fight your machine. Let it do the work for you. Let the feed teeth pull the pieces under the machine foot; all you need to do is guide them. Use the quick unpicker to hold edges together or seam allowances flat to stop movement. If you push or pull you will distort the pieces and the seam allowance will not be accurate.

Sew right to the end before removing the piece and cutting threads. This is where using leaders comes in handy. If the piece is pulled away too soon the seam allowance at the end will be narrower than at the beginning and the unit will have a bend in it, as illustrated in figure 16. This happens frequently when joining block units together.

Figure 16 Incorrectly sewn pieces

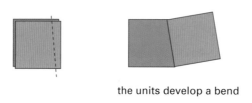

the units develop a bend

Avoid chain piecing when assembling the actual block sections together as mistakes will creep in. Use chain piecing for strip piecing, and when sewing triangles together for bias square construction, but avoid it in the actual block construction.

Follow the leader

If your machine loves to chew up fabric when beginning to sew, fold a scrap of fabric and feed this through first. Sew across it and stop at the edge. Leave the needle down in the fabric, carefully raise the pressure foot a little, position the pieces to be sewn close to the edge of the leader, lower the foot and continue sewing. When you get to the end, leave the needle down, snip off the leader from the beginning, raise the foot slightly and slide the leader against the edge. Lower the foot and keep sewing to the edge of the leader. Leave the needle in the down position, lift the pressure foot and cut away the sewn pieces from the back. Alternately you could use two leader pieces. Starting and finishing on a leader is similar to chain piecing. It eliminates a forest of threads and curtails your machine's appetite. It also helps in keeping the correct seam allowance width right to the end of the pieces being sewn together.

Pressing

PRESSING IS JUST as important as having an accurate seam allowance. I use steam all the time as it gives a crisp finish and is helpful when pressing bulky seams open. Develop a rhythm of sewing and then pressing immediately—this is very important—then opening out the seam and finger-pressing it while it is still hot, gently running your nail along the stitching. The seam will stay open, making it easy to press with the iron. Gently press on the wrong side first, then on the right side. This method stops small pleats forming along the seam allowance. The resulting unit will be completely flat. Pressing in this manner creates less stress on the strips, and tends to eliminate the bow effect that is so common with strip piecing.

All seams are pressed open unless instructed otherwise. In pressing seams to one side, surface area is actually lost. In large blocks a $\frac{1}{16}$ inch (2 mm) loss is not noticeable, but in miniatures losing the same amount is like losing $\frac{1}{4}$ inch (0.75 cm) in a large block. Pressing open distributes the seam allowances evenly across the block surface. You will also notice that even though your seam allowance was sewn the correct width, after pressing the seams on the back of a block they will be smaller, especially with the last couple of seams joining a block unit together. This is normal with miniatures.

Pressing direction for seams is indicated with arrows on block piecing diagrams—either to one side, or open.

Sashing strips

Before you start cutting fabric for sashing strips, it is always advisable to measure all your blocks first. Find the most common measurement and cut the sashing strips this length. While the exact measurements are given in the instructions for all quilts, I recommend that you always measure your blocks to avoid disappointment.

As mentioned before, some cutting instructions for sashing strips include the extra width for insurance. This only occurs where long unpieced sashing strips are used to join rows together. For quilts that have sashing strips with posts, the sashing strips are cut the correct width. Another way to handle short sashing strips, illustrated in figure 17, is to cut a strip the width of the block. Sew a block to the strip, press the seam away from the block and then trim away the excess strip, leaving the sashing strip the required finished width plus one seam allowance.

**Figure 17 Attaching blocks to sashing strips
that are in one piece**

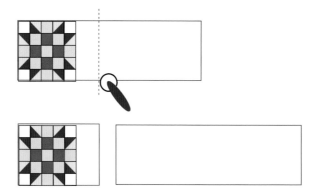

To keep vertical sashing strips in line after sewing a row of blocks to a horizontal sashing strip, make matching marks on the wrong side of the long sashing strip indicating where the vertical sashing strips intersect it, as shown in figure 18. When joining the next row of blocks to this strip, match these marks with the vertical sashing strips in the row of blocks to be joined. This applies to both straight set quilts and quilts set on point.

Figure 18 Attaching long sashing strips with matching marks

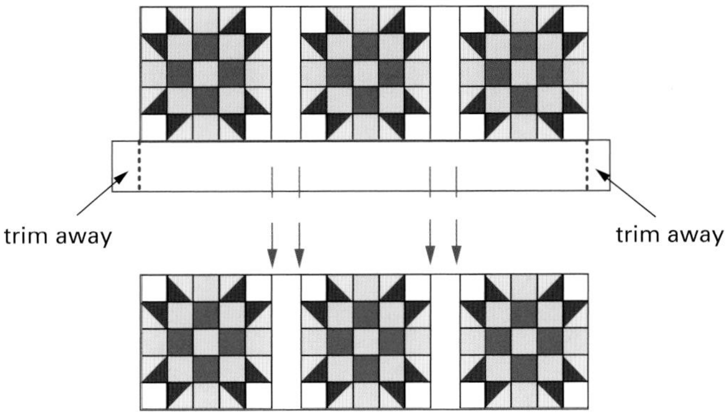

trim away   trim away

When measuring for long sashing strips, mark the required measurement onto the strip. Leave about ½ inch (1.25 cm) extending beyond each end mark and cut. This gives you a bit to play with if necessary. The excess is trimmed away after the strip has been joined to both rows of blocks.

When sewing sashing strips to the blocks or rows of blocks, have them on top, as they are easier to control.

Quilt assembly

Straight set quilts

STRAIGHT SET QUILTS have the blocks sewn together into rows, with or without sashing strips dividing them. They may be joined with unpieced strips or have sashing posts to add more interest to the design, as illustrated in figure 19.

Figure 19 Assembling straight set quilts

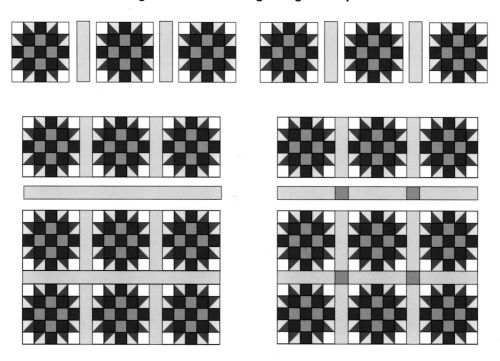

Quilts set on point

Quilts with blocks set on point require side and corner setting triangles. These are half and quarter-square triangles which are cut oversize. The excess is trimmed away after the top has been pieced together. After trimming, the quilt top will have nice straight edges and a perfect ¼ inch (0.75 cm) seam allowance on all four sides. See figure 20.

Figure 20 Assembling quilts on point set block to block

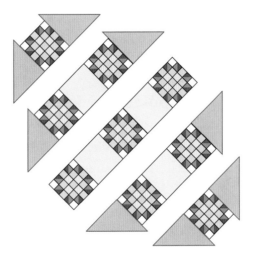

Side-setting triangles These are quarter-square triangles cut from a parent square that is cut 3½ inches (9 cm) larger than the finished size of the block. For example, if a block is 2 inches (5 cm) square, the parent square is cut 5½ inches (14 cm) square. The long leg of these triangles is on the straight grain.

Corner triangles These are half-square triangles that are cut from a parent square that is cut 2 inches (5.5 cm) larger than the finished size of the block. The long leg of these triangles is on the bias and the short legs are on the straight grain.

For the quilt projects in this book that are set on point, the sashing strips and setting triangles must be attached to the blocks in a specific order, with the corner triangles being attached last. Follow the assembly instructions given for each quilt very carefully.

Quilts set on point, block to block

The blocks are joined into rows, as seen in figure 20. The side-setting triangles are sewn to the ends of the rows. The rows are then joined together to form the quilt top. Attach the corner triangles last.

Quilts set on point with unpieced sashing strips

The sashing strips for these quilts are all cut too wide. The excess is trimmed away after sewing and pressing each strip in place. This method involves matching marks to keep the short sashing strips in line, as shown in figure 21.

**Figure 21 Assembling quilts set on point
with unpieced sashing strips**

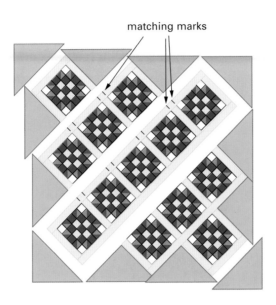

matching marks

Quilts set on point with pieced sashing strips

These are assembled in the same manner as quilts with unpieced sashing strips, but the strips are cut the exact required width. Piece the sashing strips as instructed and treat as if they were unpieced strips. See figure 22. These quilts are easier to assemble, as there is no need for matching marks. The seams of the sashing posts butt together with the sashing strip seams.

**Figure 22 Assembling quilts set on point
with pieced sashing strips**

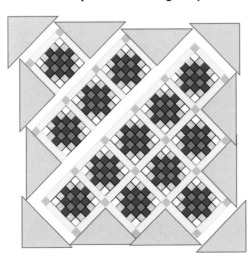

Squaring up quilts set on point

Using the long ruler, line up the vertical ¼ inch (0.75 cm) mark on the ruler on the right-hand side of the quilt, with the mark just on the outside of the sashing strip seam or the corner of the blocks, and the horizontal ¼ inch (0.75 cm) line along the top of the quilt, lining up in the same manner as for the side. Trim the excess away, leaving a ¼ inch (0.75 cm) seam allowance. See figure 23. Turn the quilt around and repeat for the remaining sides. It is now ready for the borders to be attached.

Figure 23 Squaring up a quilt set on point

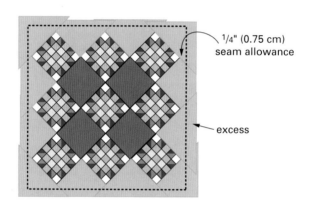

¼" (0.75 cm)
seam allowance

excess

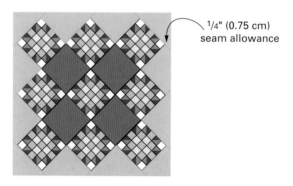

¼" (0.75 cm)
seam allowance

Borders

WITH MINIATURE QUILTS, try to keep the borders simple.

To calculate border length amounts, first measure the quilt vertically, edge to edge, through the centre. This is the length you will need for the sides. To calculate for the length of the top and bottom borders, measure the quilt horizontally through the centre, to the outer edges of the side borders. If the quilt is a little uneven, measure all four sides and work out an average size.

Inner borders or frames

In the cutting instructions for the inner borders there will be an extra ⅛ inch (0.25 cm) or more added to the width for insurance. All inner and outer borders have squared, not mitred corners.

Measure the quilt vertically through the centre, edge to edge. Mark this measurement onto a strip, leaving ½ inch (1 cm) at both ends for insurance. Cut two sections this length off the bulk of the prepared strip. See figure 24.

Figure 24 Matching marks and extra at the ends of a border strip

Fold the strips and the quilt top in half and pin mark. Matching the marks on the strips to the edges of the quilt, and to the pins, sew the sides in place. Press the seams towards the borders. Remove the excess from the ends using the straight edge of the quilt as a guide. Use the rotary cutter and ruler to do this, not scissors.

Measure the quilt horizontally through the centre, edge to edge. Measure, mark and cut in the same manner as for the sides. Sew to the top and bottom of the quilt. Press seams towards the borders. As these strips have been cut too wide, trim the excess down as instructed. This leaves nice straight edges on which to attach the outer borders. If these inner borders are to be ¼ inch (0.75 cm) finished width, trim the seam allowances down slightly after sewing and pressing each strip so the next row of stitching will not anchor them down. See figure 25.

Figure 25 Attaching inner borders

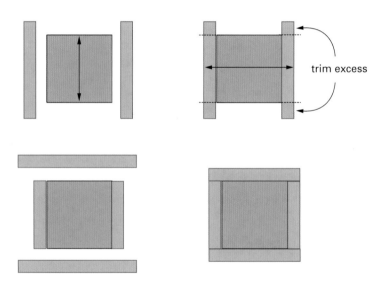

Outer borders

These are measured and attached in the same manner as the inner borders, except that the excess strip width is not trimmed away until after quilting. See figure 26.

Figure 26 Attaching outer borders

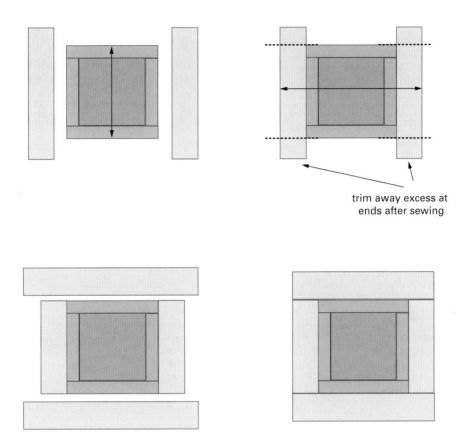

trim away excess at
ends after sewing

Assembling the layers

THE BACKING AND BATTING should be larger than the quilt top. I find that an extra 2 inches (5 cm) all round is enough for miniatures. Make sure each layer is smooth, especially the top. Press gently; this will be the last time.

Place the backing fabric right side facing down on a firm surface. Place the batting over this, smoothing out any wrinkles, then place the quilt on top.

Because I machine quilt all my miniatures, I pin baste them, usually in the centre of each block and around the inner border if there is one, and around the outside edge of the outer border.

If you intend to hand quilt, baste with a neutral coloured thread, and avoid bulky seam junctions.

Quilting

LESS IS BEST WHEN it comes to quilting. Miniatures that are over-quilted do not lie flat, and can become distorted. Depending on the quilt design, I find that quilting in the ditch around each block if there are sashing strips, and in the ditch around the inner and outer borders, is generally enough. If the quilt has been put together block to block, a simple all-over design can be used. Always begin in the centre of the quilt and work outwards. Remove the pins as you get to them. Pull the top threads to the back and tie off as you go. After quilting the centre you may have to reposition the pins holding the border layers in place.

Most of the outer borders are around 3½ to 4 inches (9 to 10.5 cm) wide after squaring up, so there is room for a simple pattern or free-motion quilting. Do not quilt right to the edges, as you will lose some of the design when the quilt is squared up and bound. If you intend to hand quilt using a frame, attach wide calico strips to all four sides, making the quilt wide enough to fit in a small frame comfortably. Lengthen the stitches on the machine so the strips are easily removed after quilting.

Free-motion quilting is very addictive and it can be as heavy or as light as you wish. I use it all the time on my quilts as you can obtain wonderful unexpected effects. Just be aware that if the quilting in the centre is light, you must also quilt lightly in the borders or the centre will 'pop' out and the quilt will not lie flat. For free-motion quilting you will need a darning foot for the machine and need to be able to lower the feed teeth.

After quilting is completed, neaten the edges of the quilt ready for the bindings. Square the quilt up in the same manner as described on page 34, leaving the borders the required width. The required measurement line on the ruler is placed on the edges of the pieced areas or the outer edge of the inner borders.

Binding

BINDING WIDTHS CAN vary according to the size of the quilt. I use a single layer straight grain binding. Bindings must be full, and the edges of the quilt sandwich must rest right in the fold. I achieve this by making the seam allowance the required finished width of the bindings. The binding strips are all cut wider than necessary so there is enough seam allowance to get a good turn-under on the back before hand sewing down. When attaching them with a ¼ inch seam, make the seam allowance slightly wider, about ⁵⁄₁₆ inch unless instructed otherwise. In the instructions this is mentioned as a generous ¼ inch. (The extra does not apply in metric measurements, as an 0.75 cm seam will give a nice size binding.)

Bindings are measured and attached in the same manner as borders.

To get nice squared corners on the bindings, try the method illustrated in figure 27. Measure and attach the side bindings. Hand sew down in place. When measuring for the top and bottom bindings, add an extra 1½ inch (3.75 cm); this is for turning the ends of the strips around so that the corners are completely enclosed. Mark halfway on the edges of both the quilt and the binding strips. Match the marks and pin the binding in place. Turn the ends of the bindings around to the back of the quilt and pin in place. Sew the bindings from edge to edge. Turn the binding to the back, pulling up the corner folds, which will then enclose the raw edges of the side strips. Turn under the seam allowance and hand sew down. I use this method for both large and small quilts and end up with perfect corners every time. Well— almost every time.

Figure 27 Attaching binding

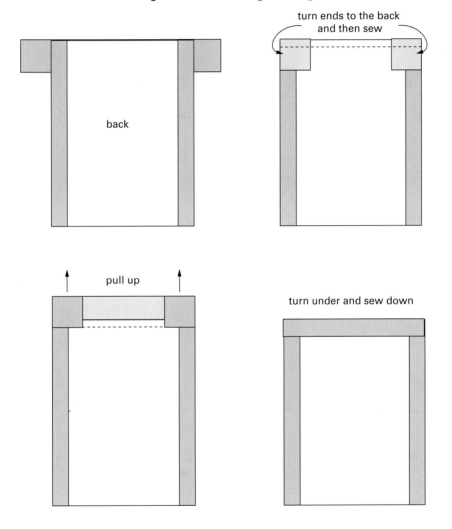

Hanging your treasures

THERE ARE LOTS of different ways to display miniature quilts. They can be hung on the wall, placed in a miniature quilt frame or draped over miniature beds. The unbound top can be framed and hung, or quilted and then framed. Both of these can look really great.

For hanging, sew small loops to the back of the quilt, and thread a decorative rod through the loops. Another way is to attach small pieces of the fluffy half of Velcro to the back of the quilt; the corresponding scratchy bits can be attached to a rod covered with fabric. Decorative wire hangers and mini pegs are other options.

Whatever method you use, just like big quilts miniatures need to be kept out of strong light. Dust can be shaken off and if necessary they can be washed. Treat them with the same amount of care as you would their larger cousins, and they will last for future generations to admire.

PROJECTS

Nautical Cats

Quilt size 16 x 16 inches (40.5 x 40.5 cm)
Block size 3 inches (8 cm)

I had a lot of fun with this quilt. It is made from scraps and the border
fabric features marvellous cats. This is an easy quilt to start with.

Requirements

Sewing machine and accessories
Rotary cutter, mat and rulers
Bias square ruler
Scissors, pins, quick unpicker and tape measure
Thread:
>   *neutral colour for piecing*
>   *colour to match border fabric*
>   *gold and silver metallics for quilting*

Background fabric: 10 inches (26 cm) for pieces A, B and D
Bright fabric scraps:
>   *boat hulls, 4¼ x 1¼ inch (11.5 x 3.5 cm) rectangles of*
>   *nine different fabrics. C.*
>   *sails, 5 inch (10 cm) squares of at least nine different fabrics. F.*
>   *water fabric: 12 x 4½ inches (30 x 12 cm) blue. E.*

Border fabric, cats: 6 inches (16 cm)
Binding: 3 inches (8 cm)
Backing fabric: fat quarter
Batting: fat quarter

Cutting

Background fabric

Cut one strip 1¾ inch (5.25 cm) wide and cut fifteen 1¾ inch (5.25 cm) squares.
Cut diagonally once to yield thirty half-square triangles. A.

Cut one strip 2 inch (5.5 cm) wide and cut twelve 2 inch (5.5 cm) squares. Cut
diagonally once. Keep these separate from the other triangles. D.

Cut one strip 1¼ inch (3.5 cm) wide and cut eighteen 1¼ x 2 inch (3.5 x 5.5 cm)
rectangles. B.

Put the rest aside for the sashing strips and inner borders.

Block A

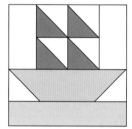

Block B

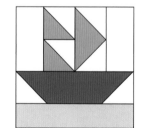

Water fabric

Cut three 1¼ inch (3.5 cm) strips and cut nine 3½ x 1¼ inch (9.5 x 3.5 cm)
rectangles. E.

Boat hull fabric

Use the nine pre-cut rectangles. The ends of these are trimmed away. Place a rectangle, right side facing up, on the cutting mat. Position the bias square ruler with the diagonal marked line running along the top edge of the fabric and the point of the ruler at the top right-hand corner (diagram 1a). Cut away the corner. Turn the strip over and trim away the other corner in the same manner (diagram 1b). Do this to all nine rectangles.

Diagram 1 Cutting the boat hulls

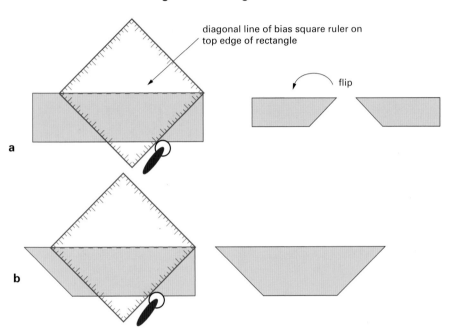

Sail fabric

I suggest that you select the desired sail fabric for one block at a time. Construct the block, then go on to the next one.

Boat A For one boat cut two 1 ¾ inch (5.25 cm) squares. Cut these diagonally once to yield four half-square triangles. F.

Boat B For one boat cut one 1 ¾ inch (5.25 cm) square. Cut diagonally once to yield two half-square triangles. F.

Cut one 2 ¾ inch (7.5 cm) square. Cut diagonally twice to yield four quarter-square triangles. G. You will only need one of these per block. Put the other three aside.

Construction

Please look at the quilt photo before you begin to put the blocks together, as I made some boats with their sails reversed. The instructions below for boats A and B have the sails going in the same direction, but you can change this to follow the photo if you wish.

Boat A

Sew a half-square triangle D to both ends of the boat fabric trimmed rectangle, following diagram 2. These triangles are too big. Centre the trimmed edges on the triangles. Sew, press towards the triangles. Use the rotary cutter and bias square ruler to trim the unit down to 3½ x 1¼ inches (9.5 x 3.5 cm).

Diagram 2 Steps in sewing boat hull A and B

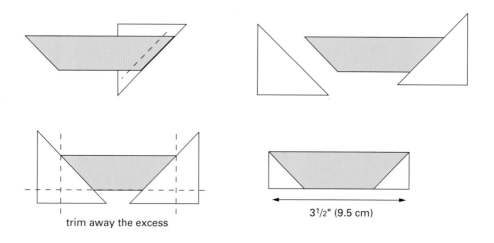

trim away the excess

3½" (9.5 cm)

Join the four 1¾ inch (5.25 cm) sail fabric half-square triangles, F, to four of the background half-square triangles, A. Press seams open and trim down into 1¼ inch (3.5 cm) bias squares. (If you are working in metric measurements, trim all seam allowances down to 0.5 cm from now on.)

Lay out the pieces as shown in diagram 3 and join together. Press in the direction of the arrows.

Diagram 3 Assembling block A

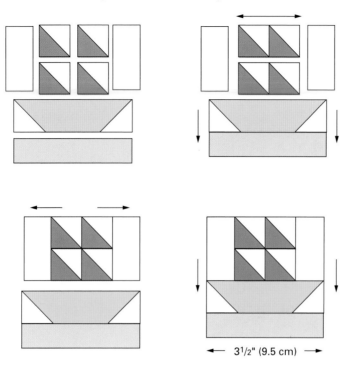

3¹/₂" (9.5 cm)

Boat B

Sew two D half-square triangles to one of the quarter-square triangles, G. See diagram 4. These are sewn in the same manner as for the boat section, centring the edges of the quarter-square triangle. Press seams open. These triangles are too big. Excess is trimmed after sewing, leaving the sail unit 1¼ x 2 inch (3.5 x 5.5 cm). Make sure there is a ¼ inch (0.75 cm) allowance at the bottom of the unit. (If you are working in metric measurements, trim all seam allowances down to 0.5 cm from now on.)

Diagram 4 Boat B—large sail

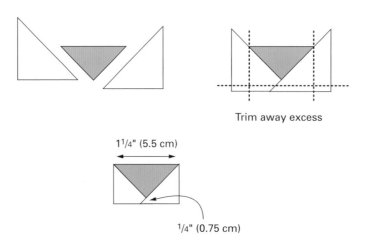

Trim away excess

1¹/₄" (5.5 cm)

¹/₄" (0.75 cm)

Follow the piecing diagram (figure 5) and assemble the block. Press in the direction of the arrows.

Diagram 5 Assembling block B

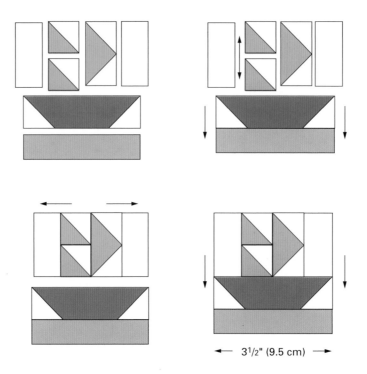

3¹/₂" (9.5 cm)

Make nine blocks, three of block B and six of block A. They will measure 3½ inches (9.5 cm) square at this stage.

Quilt assembly

Quilt top

From the remaining background fabric cut one 1 inch (2.75 cm) wide strip and cut twelve 1 x 3½ inch (2.75 x 9.5 cm) sashing strips.

From the leftover scraps, cut four 1 inch (2.75 cm) squares. Use these and six of the sashing strips to form two pieced sashing strips, as shown in diagram 6. Press seams away from the squares.

Diagram 6
make 2

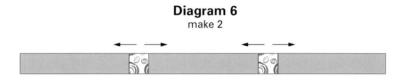

Refer to figures 19 and 20 on page 30—31.

Lay out the blocks in three rows of three, referring to quilt photo for block placement. (If you are working in metric measurements, trim all seam allowances down to 0.5 cm from now on.)

Press all seams towards the sashing strips.

Sew a sashing strip to the right-hand side of the first two blocks in each row. Press.

Join the blocks together to form three rows.

Sew a pieced sashing strip to the bottom of the first two rows. Press.

Join the rows together to form the top.

Borders

Refer to figures 25 and 26 on page 36–37.

Inner border Cut two 1⅛ inch (3 cm) wide strips from the background fabric.

Measure and attach the inner borders. Trim these down to ¾ inch (2 cm) wide. (If you are working in metric measurements, trim all seam allowances down to 0.5 cm from now on.) The inner border pieces will be ½ inch (1.25 cm) finished width.

Outer border Cut two 3 inch (8 cm) wide strips. Measure and attach in the same manner as for the inner borders. Press seams towards the borders.

Quilting

Assemble the three layers. Pin baste and quilt a design of your choice. I quilted the top with an overall meandering pattern, taking it through all sashing strips and out into the borders.

After quilting, neaten the borders so they are 2½ inches (6.5 cm) wide. Refer to page 34.

Binding

Refer to diagram 27 on page 41.

Cut two 1½ inch (4 cm) wide strips from the binding fabric. Measure and attach using a ¼ inch (0.75 cm) seam.

Diagram 7 Quilt assembly

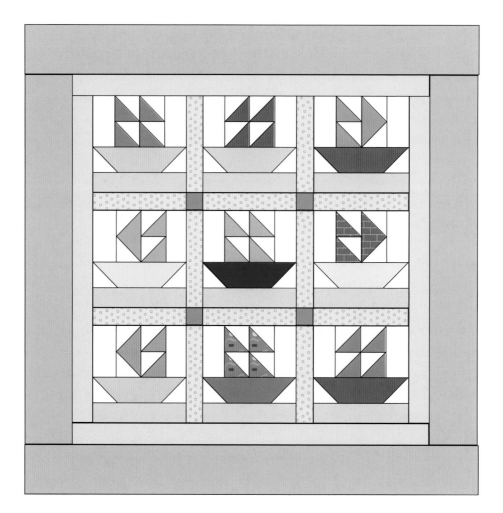

Irregular Sawtooth

Quilt size 15½ x 15½ inches (39.5 x 39.5 cm)
Block size 2 inches (5 cm)

This is a true scrap quilt in which I used leftover blue and jade scraps and background fabrics. The only fabrics I had to buy were for the borders, binding and backing.

Requirements

Sewing machine and accessories
Rotary cutter, mat and rulers
Bias square ruler
Scissors, pins, quick unpicker and tape measure
Thread:
> *neutral colour for piecing*
> *navy blue*
> *thread for quilting to match background fabric*

Background 1 fabric: 8 x 22 inch (20 x 56 cm) white or cream for the block piecing. A and B.
Background 2 fabric: 22 x 6 inch (56 x 15 cm) for setting squares and triangles
Eight assorted blue fabrics: 2 x 8 inches (5 x 22 cm) piece of each. C.
Jade green fabric/s: nine 1½ inch (4 cm) squares for the block centres, from one fabric or nine different ones. D.
Inner border and binding fabric: 12 x 22 inches (30 x 56 cm) jade green
Outer border fabric: blue fat quarter
Backing fabric and batting: fat quarter

Cutting

Background fabric 1

Cut two strips 1 inch (2.75 cm) wide. Cut into thirty-six 1 inch (2.75 cm) squares. A.

Cut two strips 1½ inch (4.5 cm) wide. Cut into thirty-six 1½ inch (4.5 cm) squares. Cut these diagonally once to form half-square triangles, working as shown in diagram 1. Bias squares. B.

Block diagram

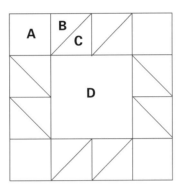

Diagram 1 Cutting background squares on the diagonal with the bulk of the strip moved away slightly

Blue fabric

From each of the eight different fabrics cut five 1½ inch (4.5 cm) squares. Cut diagonally once to form half-square triangles. Bias squares. C.

Jade green fabric

Cut nine 1½ inch (4 cm) squares. D.

Block construction

Refer to page 19.

Sew each assorted blue half-square triangle to each of the background 1 half-square triangles, press the seams open and trim down into 1 inch (2.75 cm) bias squares. You will need seventy-two.

To make one block, lay out the pieces and follow diagram 2. Have one bias square from each blue fabric in each block and vary the positions of the blue fabrics in each block. Press seams in the direction of the arrows. (If you are working in metric measurements, trim all seam allowances down to 0.5 cm from now on.)

Make eight more blocks. The blocks will measure 2½ inches (6.5 cm) square at this point.

Block assembly

Diagram 2 Block assembly

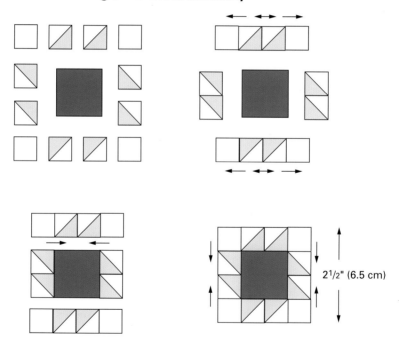

2¹/₂" (6.5 cm)

Background fabric 2
Side-setting triangles Cut two 5½ inch (14 cm) squares. Cut diagonally twice.
Corners Cut two 4 inch (10.5 cm) squares. Cut diagonally once.
Setting squares Cut four 2½ inch (6.5 cm) squares.

Quilt assembly

Quilt top
Arrange the blocks in a pleasing order with the setting squares, as shown in diagram 3.

Diagram 3 Quilt assembly

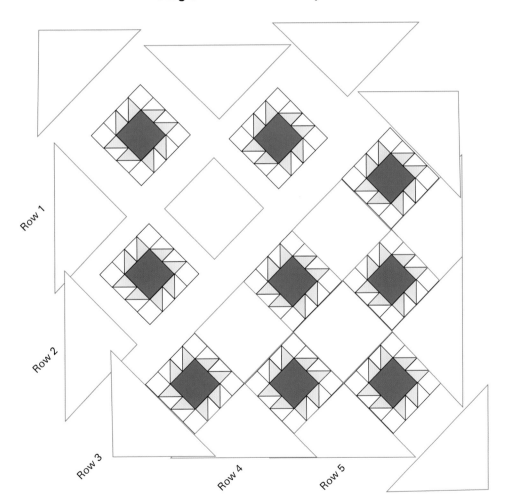

Join the blocks and setting squares together to form rows 2, 3 and 4. Press seams towards the setting squares.

Sew the side-setting triangles in place on rows 1 and 5. Press seams towards the triangles.

Join the rows together to form the top. Press these seams open.

Sew the corner triangles in place. Press seams towards the triangles.

Refer to diagram 23 on page 34 and square up the quilt, leaving ½ inch (1.5 cm) extending on all four sides.

Borders
Refer to diagrams 25 and 26 on page 35–36.

Inner border From the jade green fabric cut four 1 inch (2.75 cm) strips.

Measure and sew a strip to each side of the quilt top. Trim these seam allowances down to ⅛ inch (0.5 cm) wide.

Measure and attach the top and bottom strips and trim as before.

Trim all four inner border strips down to ½ inch (1.5 cm) wide.

Outer border Cut four strips 4 inches (10 cm) wide.

Measure and attach. Press seams towards the borders.

Quilting
Assemble the three layers and pin baste in each block and in the inner border.

Free-motion quilt in each of the setting squares and side-setting triangles. Smooth the outer borders and pin about ½ inch (1 cm) in from the edges. Quilt a design of your choice in the outer borders.

Neaten the edges of the quilt so the borders measure 3 inches (8 cm) wide.

Binding
Refer to diagram 27 on page 41.

Cut four 1½ inch (4 cm) wide strips. Measure and attach using a ¼ inch (0.75 cm) seam.

Four-Patch Grid

Quilt size 21¼ x 21¼ inches (54 x 54 cm)
Block size 2½ inches (6.25 cm)

This quilt is constructed using basic strip-piecing techniques. Using the same dark blue in the blocks and sashing strips creates a strong grid.

Requirements

Sewing machine and accessories
Rotary cutter, mat and rulers
Bias square ruler
Scissors, pins, quick unpicker and tape measure
Thread:
>   *neutral for piecing*
>   *dark blue*

Fabric measurements based on 44 inch (112 cm) width:
>   *background: fat quarter*
>   *dark blue: 24 inches (60 cm)*
>   *yellow: 4 x 22 inch (10 x 56 cm) rectangle*
>   *orange: 4 x 22 inch (10 x 56 cm) rectangle*
>   *backing: 26 inch (66 cm) square*

Batting: 26 inch (66 cm) square

Cutting

Dark blue fabric

For the borders and binding cut two strips 5 inches (13 cm) wide, and three strips 1½ inch (4 cm) wide.

From the remaining fabric cut the following.

- One strip 1⅛ inch (3 cm) wide. Cut in half to yield two strips. Strip unit A.
- Two strips 1½ inch (4 cm) wide. Cut into fifty-six 1 x 1½ inch (2.75 x 4 cm) segments. E.

Put the remaining fabric aside for the sashing strips.

Yellow fabric

Cut three strips 1⅛ x 22 inches (3 x 56 cm) long. Strip unit B.

Orange fabric

Cut two strips 1⅛ x 22 inches (3 x 56 cm) long. Strip unit C.

Put the rest aside for the sashing posts.

Background fabric

Cut seven strips 1⅛ inch (3 cm) wide. Strip units A, B and C.

Cut two 6 inch (15.25 cm) squares. Cut diagonally twice. Side-setting triangles. Put aside for later.

Cut two 4½ inch (11.75 cm) squares. Cut diagonally once. Corner triangles. Put aside for later.

Block diagrams

unit B		unit B
E		
unit A		unit C
	D	
unit C		unit A
unit B		unit B

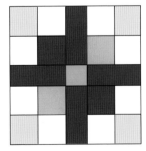

Block construction

Refer to page 16.

Diagram 1 Strip-pieced units

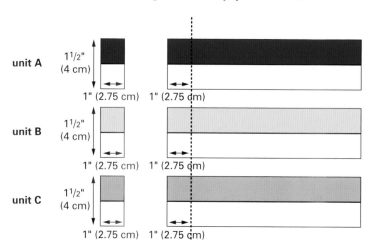

Strip-pieced units

Following diagram 1:

Unit A With right sides together sew the two dark blue and two background 1 ⅛ inch (3 cm) strips together. Press seams open and trim both strips down to ¾ inch (2 cm) from seam line to edge. Cut into twenty-six 1 x 1½ inch (2.75 x 4 cm) segments.

Unit B With right sides together sew three yellow and three background 1 ⅛ inch (3 cm) strips together. Press and trim as for unit A. Cut into fifty-two 1 x 1½ inch (2.75 x 4 cm) segments.

Unit C With right sides together sew two orange and two background 1 ⅛ inch (3 cm) strips together. Press and trim as for unit A. Cut into twenty-six 1 x 1½ inch (2.75 m x 4 cm) segments.

Four-patch units

Following diagram 2:

Group 1 Assemble twenty-six four-patch units using the segments from the strip-pieced units A and B. Press seams open.

Group 2 Assemble twenty-six four-patch units using segments from strip-pieced units B and C.

Diagram 2 Four-patch construction

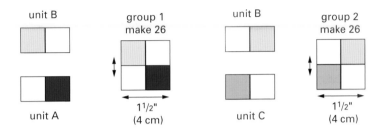

Block assembly

Arrange pieces for one block following diagram 3. (If you are working in metric measurements, trim all seam allowances down to 0.5 cm from now on.) I suggest you make one block at a time, as it is very easy to rotate the four-patch units incorrectly. Press seams in the direction of the arrows. Make thirteen blocks. They will measure 3 inches (7.75 cm) at this stage.

Diagram 3 Block piecing

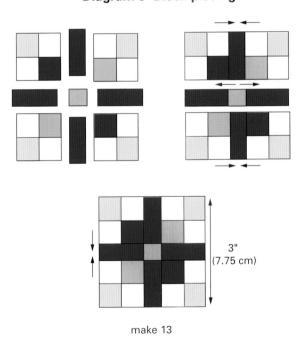

make 13

Quilt assembly

Sashing strips

These are cut the correct width.

Diagram 4 Pieced sashing strips

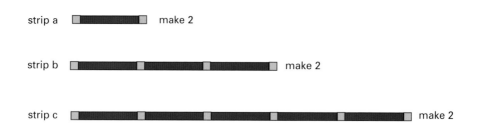

Dark blue Cut three 1 inch (2.75 cm) strips. Cut into thirty-six 1 x 3 inch (2.75 x 7.75 cm) segments.

Orange Cut two 1 inch (2.75 cm) strips. Cut twenty-four 1 inch (2.75 cm) squares. D.

Assemble six sashing strip units (two each of a, b and c) as shown in diagram 4. Press seams towards the strips, away from the squares.

Quilt top

Lay out the blocks on your work area. Note that four of the inner blocks are rotated so the orange 'steps' run horizontally instead of vertically.

Referring to figure 22 on page 33 (assembling a quilt set on point with pieced sashing strips), assemble the quilt top. Press all seams towards the sashing strips. (If you are working in metric measurements, trim all seam allowances down to 0.5 cm.)

Sew an unpieced strip to the right-hand side of each block.

Sew an unpieced strip to the left-hand side of the first block in each row.

Sew one strip a to the top of row 1 and the other to the bottom of row 5.

Sew one strip b to the top of row 2 and the other to the bottom of row 4.

Sew the two c strips to the top and bottom of row 3.

Position the side-setting triangles at the ends of the rows as shown. Sew and press seams towards the sashing strips. Join the rows together and press seams towards sashing strips. Attach the corner triangles last and press seams towards them.

Refer to figure 23 on page 34 and square up the quilt, leaving a ¼ inch (0.75 cm) seam allowance on all four sides.

Diagram 5 Quilt assembly

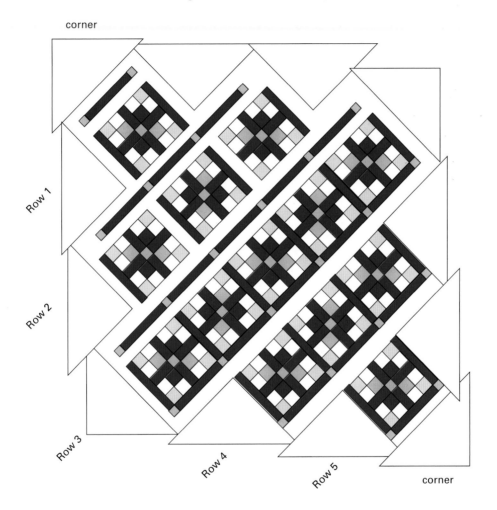

Borders
Refer to figures 25 and 26 on page 36–37.

Using the two pre-cut 5 inch (13 cm) wide border strips, measure the top vertically through the centre, edge to edge, and cut one strip this length off both border strips. The remaining pieces of the strips are for the top and bottom.

Sew the borders to the sides of the quilt. Measure and attach the top and bottom borders. Press towards the borders.

Finishing

Refer to pages 38 and 39.

Assemble the three layers and pin baste. Quilt as desired. If you quilt lightly in the centre, make sure the border quilting is light as well or the quilt will not lie flat.

After quilting, trim the borders down to 4¼ inches (11 cm) wide.

Binding

Refer to figure 27 on page 41.

Use the three pre-cut dark blue 1½ inch (4 cm) strips. Cut one in half for the sides and use the two long ones for the top and bottom. Measure and attach to the quilt using a generous ¼ inch (0.75 cm) seam, binding the sides first, then the top and bottom.

Mother's Choice

Quilt size approx. 20½ x 20½ inches (52 x 52 cm)
Block size 2½ inches (6.25 cm)

This quilt has been constructed using brown, orange and beige fabrics.

This is a great little scrap quilt and is assembled fairly quickly.

Photograph has contrasting binding

Requirements

Sewing machine and accessories
Rotary cutter, mat and rulers
Bias square ruler
Scissors, pins, quick unpicker and tape measure
Thread:
neutral colour for piecing
matching thread for borders
thread for machine quilting
Fabric measurements based on 44 inch (112 cm) width;
amounts are generous:
blocks: total of 16 assorted beige, yellow and brown fabrics,
each 12 x 4 inches (30 x 10 cm)
background: 14 inches (36 cm)
border+binding: 14 inches (36 cm)
backing: 22 x 22 inches (56 x 56 cm)
Batting: 22 x 22 inches (56 x 56 cm)

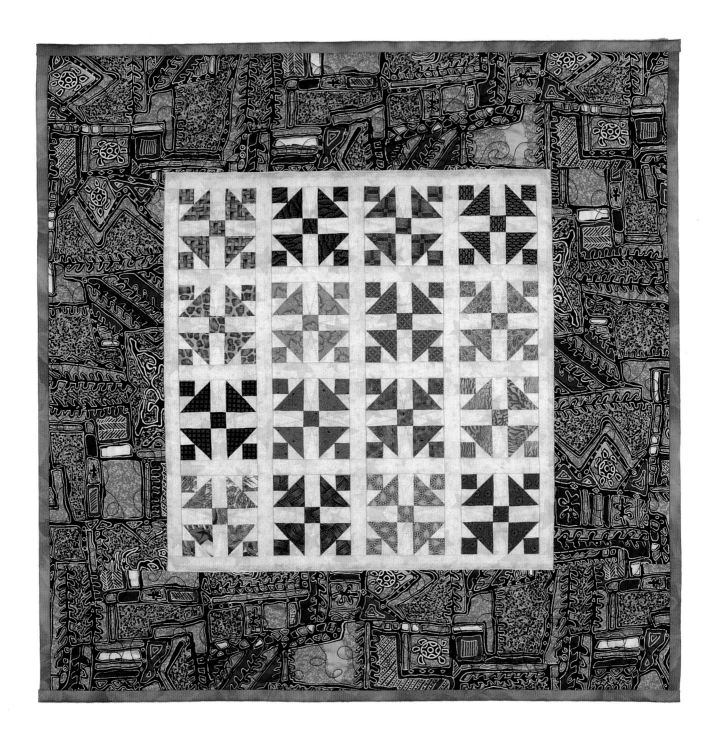

Cutting

Background fabric

Cut two strips 1½ inch (4 cm) wide, cut into sixty-four rectangles, 1 x 1½ inch (2.75 x 4 cm). A.

Cut two strips 1⅜ inch (3.75 cm) wide, cut into sixty-four 1⅜ inch (3.75 cm) squares.

Cut these diagonally once to yield 128 half-square triangles. D.

Refer to page 19 for a quick way of cutting these.

Assorted fabrics

From each fabric cut the following:

- One strip 2¼ x 12 inches (6.25 x 30 cm) and four 2¼ inch (6.25 cm) squares. B.
- One strip 1 inch (2.75 cm) wide and cut five 1 inch (2.75 cm) squares. C.

Block diagrams

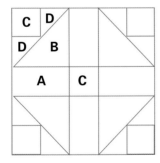 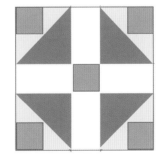

Assembling one block

Sew two 1 ⅜ inch (3.75 cm) background half-square triangles to each of four 1 inch (2.75 cm) squares from one of the assorted fabrics. Make sure the edges are parallel (see diagram 1). Press the seams open

Diagram 1 Assembling the pieced triangle units

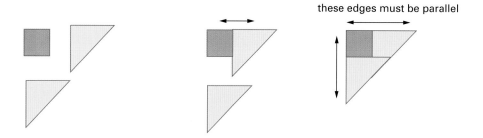

Referring back to page 23, sew these four triangle units to the four 2¼ inch (6.25 cm) squares of the same fabric (see diagram 2). Press the seams away from the triangle units. (If you are working in metric measurements, trim all seam allowances down to 0.5 cm from now on.) Trim away the excess square at the back, then use the bias square ruler to trim the units down to 1½ inch (4 cm) square.

Diagram 2 Assembling the block unit

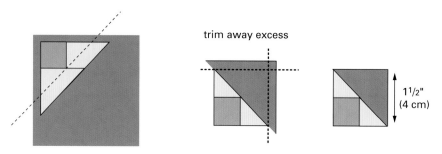

Follow piecing diagram 3 and assemble the block. Press in the direction of the arrows.

Construct sixteen blocks. They will measure 3 inches (7.75 cm) at this stage.

Diagram 3 Assembling the block

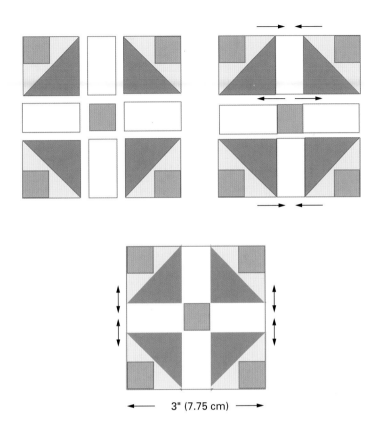

3" (7.75 cm)

Quilt assembly

Arrange the blocks into four rows of four beside your machine.

Sashing strips

Refer to page 28. The sashing strips are cut too wide. Trim them down to
¾ inch (2 cm) wide after sewing and pressing. Press all seams towards the
sashing strips. (If you are working in metric measurements, trim all seam
allowances down to 0.5 cm.)

Cut four strips 1 ⅛ inch (3 cm) wide from the background fabric.

Cut twelve 3 x 1 ⅛ inch (7.75 x 3 cm) sashing strips. Sew these to the right-
hand side of the first three blocks in each row (diagram 4).

Diagram 4 Attaching sashing strips

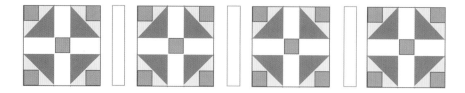

Quilt top

Join the blocks together to form four rows of four blocks. Measure the length of the rows and add ½ inch (1.25 cm) to this. Cut five strips to this measurement. Sew one strip to the bottom of the first three rows. Trim the strips down and the excess at the ends. Make sashing strip matching marks on all three strips where the vertical sashing strips intersect, as in diagram 5.

Diagram 5 Attaching horizontal sashing strips

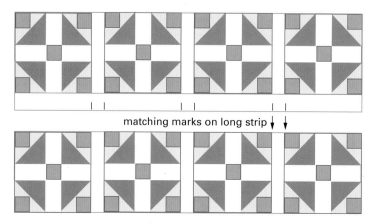

matching marks on long strip

Join the rows together, matching the marks and sashing strips. Press.

Sew the two remaining strips to the top and bottom rows. Press. Do not trim these seams down unless you are working in metric measurements.

Measure the quilt vertically through the centre, edge to edge, and cut two 1⅛ inch (3 cm) wide strips this length. Sew these to the sides. Trim the seams down to 0.5 cm if using metric measurements. Press towards the side strips and then trim these and the top and bottom ones down to ¾ inch (2 cm) wide.

Borders

Refer to figures 25 and 26 on page 36–37.

Press all seams towards the borders.

Cut two strips 4½ inches (11.5 cm) wide. Cut in half.

Measure, mark and attach the top and bottom borders. Press.

Measure, mark and attach the side borders. Press.

Assemble the three layers together and pin baste.

Quilting

Quilt in the ditch around each block and then quilt a design of your choice in the border, making it no wider than 3¼ inches (9.5 cm).

After quilting, neaten the border edges to measure 4 inches (10 cm) wide.

Binding

Refer to figure 27 on page 41.

From the remaining border fabric cut two strips 1½ inch (4 cm) wide. Cut in half.

Measure and sew in place, using a generous ¼ inch (0.75 cm) seam.

Diagram 6 Top ready for the outer borders

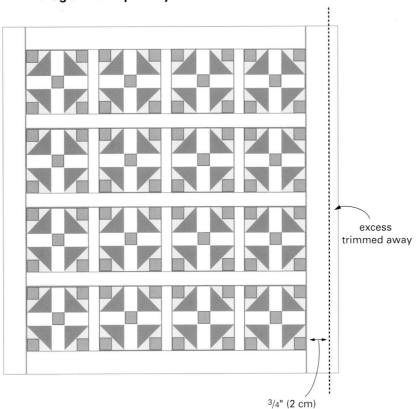

excess trimmed away

3/4" (2 cm)

Nine-Patch Stars

Quilt size approx. 16 x 19½ inches (34 x 40 cm)
Block size 2½ inches (6.25 cm);
12 blocks set 3 x 4 with sashing strips and posts

This is a very traditional pattern. The use of strong-coloured fabrics makes the quilt glow. It is a good pattern for trying out your own fabric combinations. Go for it!

Requirements

Sewing machine and accessories
Rotary cutter, mat and rulers
Bias square ruler
Scissors, pins, quick unpicker and tape measure
Thread:
 neutral colour for piecing
 red and blue for quilting
Fabric, measurements based on 44 inch (112 cm) width:
 background: 8 inches (20 cm)
 dark blue: 12 inches (30 cm)
 orange: fat quarter
 borders and binding: red, 14 inches (36 cm)
 backing: 24 x 22 inches (62 x 56 cm)
Batting: 24 x 22 inches (62 x 56 cm)

Cutting

Background fabric

Cut a 6 inch (16 cm) wide strip. Cut this strip into a 26 inch (73 cm) length. Bias squares. B. Put to one side.

From the end of the above section, cut three strips 1 inch (2.75 cm) wide and cut into forty-eight
1 inch (2.75 cm) squares. A.

Dark blue fabric

Cut two strips 1 ⅛ inch (3 cm) wide. Cut in half to yield four strips. C. Put one strip aside; it can be used for one of the inner borders.
Cut another strip 1 ⅛ inch (3 cm) wide for the inner borders.
Cut a 6 inch (16 cm) wide strip. Cut off a 26 inch (73 cm) length. Bias squares. B. Put to one side. The remainder of the strip will be used for sashing strips.

Orange fabric

Cut three strips 1 ⅛ inch (3 cm) wide. C.
Cut four 1 inch (2.75 cm) strips and cut sixty-six 1 inch (2.75 cm) squares. Six of these are for the sashing posts, the rest are for the block piecing. D and E. Double the strips for quicker cutting.

Block diagrams

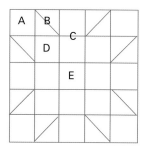 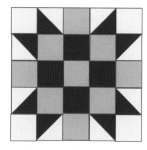

Construction

Strip units

Refer to page 16.

Sew the three orange and blue 1⅛ inch (3 cm) strips, right sides together, to form three strip units. C. See diagram 1. Press the seams open. Trim the strips so they measure ¾ inch (2 cm) wide from seam allowance to edge. Cut these into forty-eight 1½ x 1 inch (4 x 2.75 cm) segments.

Diagram 1 Strip units

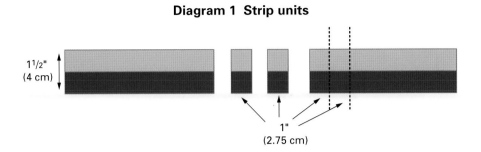

1½"
(4 cm)

1"
(2.75 cm)

Bias squares

Refer to page 20.

Place the background and blue 6 x 26 inch (16 x 73 cm) sections, right sides together and press.

Cut twelve pairs of bias strips 1 ⅛ inch (3.25 cm) wide. Sew along both long edges and press.

Using the 1 inch (2.75 cm) marks on the bias square, cut ninety-six 1 inch (2.75 cm) triangles. Make sure you leave the ⅛ inch (0.5 cm) on the left-hand sides when cutting. (For the metric version, make sure this amount is no larger than 0.5 cm or you will not get eight triangles from each strip.) Press the seams open and trim into 1 inch (2.75 cm) bias squares. If necessary, cut extra pairs of strips from the left over corner triangles. B.

Block assembly

If you are working in metric measurements, trim the seam allowances down to 0.5 cm. Assemble forty-eight corner units as shown in diagram 2. Press in the direction of the arrows.

Diagram 2 Corner units
make 48

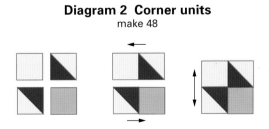

Assemble the block following diagram 3. Make twelve blocks. They will measure 3 inches (7.75 cm) at this stage.

Diagram 3 Block construction
make 12 blocks

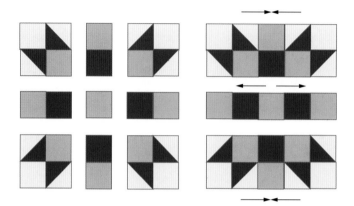

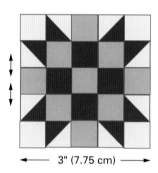

3" (7.75 cm)

Quilt assembly

Sashing strips

These are cut the required width.

Use the leftover end of the 6 inch (16 cm) blue strip, cut three strips 1 inch (2.75 cm) wide. Cut them into seventeen 3 x 1 inch (7.75 x 2.75 cm) sashing strips.

Using nine of these and the six orange 1 inch (2.75 cm) squares, assemble the three pieced sashing strips as shown in diagram 4. Press all seams towards the sashing strips.

Diagram 4 Pieced sashing strips
make 3

Quilt top

Lay out the blocks in four rows of three, following the quilt assembly diagram, and assemble the top. (If you are working in metric measurements, trim all seam allowances down to 0.5 cm.) Press all seams towards the sashing strips.

Sew a sashing strip to the right-hand side of the first two blocks in each row.

Join the blocks into four rows.

Sew a pieced sashing strip to the bottom of the first three rows.

Join the rows together.

Borders

Refer to figures 25 and 26 on page 36–37.

Inner border Using the pre-cut 1⅛ inch (3 cm) wide blue strips, measure and cut two strips for the sides. Sew and press. (If you are working in metric measurements, trim the seam allowances down to 0.5 cm.)

Repeat for the top and bottom.

Trim all four borders down to ¾ inch (2 cm) wide.

Outer border Cut two strips of the red fabric 4 inches (10.5 cm) wide. Cut in half to yield four strips. Measure and attach in the same manner as for the inner borders. Press the top well.

Diagram 5 Quilt assembly

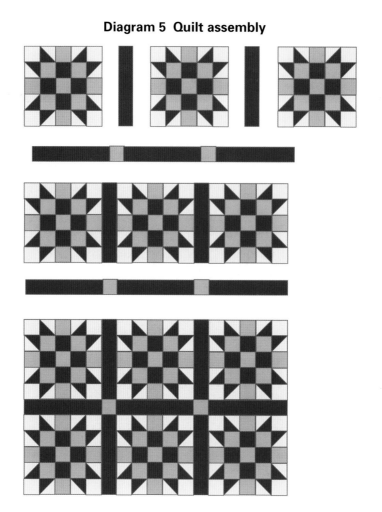

Quilting

Assemble the three layers and pin baste in the centre of each block and in the inner border.

Using a thread to match the background fabric, quilt in the ditch around each block. Change to blue thread and quilt in the ditch in the outer border seam. Change thread again to match the border fabric and quilt a design of your choice.

Neaten the edges of the borders so they measure 3¼ inches (8.5 cm) wide.

Binding

Refer to figure 27 on page 41.

From the remaining orange fabric cut two strips 1½ inch (4 cm) wide. Cut in half.

Measure and attach the bindings in place, using a generous ¼ inch (0.75 cm) seam.

Rolling Along

Quilt size 20¾ x 20¾ inches (53 x 53 cm)
Block size 3 inches (7.5 cm); 9 blocks set on point with setting squares

This quilt would have to be one of my favourites. The simple pattern and the combination of orange and purple has resulted in a sophisticated little quilt. The blocks appear to float over the surface.

Requirements

Sewing machine and accessories
Rotary cutter, mat and rulers
Bias square ruler
Scissors, pins, quick unpicker and tape measure
Thread:
to match background fabric for piecing and quilting
purple for attaching outer borders and quilting
Fabric, measurements based on 44 inch (112 cm) width:
background: 12 inches (30 cm)
bright purple: fat quarter
orange: fat quarter
borders and binding: 14 inches (35 cm)
backing: 25 inches (64 cm) square
Batting: 25 inches (64 cm) square

Cutting

Background fabric

Cut the fabric in half to yield two 12 x 22 inch (30 x 56 cm) sections. Put one of these away for the side-setting triangles.

From the other section cut the following:

- Three strips 1 ⅛ inch (3 cm) wide. D.
- Two strips 1 inch (2.75 cm) wide. Cut into thirty-six 1 inch (2.75 cm) squares. B.
- Three strips 1½ inch (4.5 cm) wide. A.

Bright purple fabric

Cut three strips 1½ inch (4.5 cm) wide. A.
Cut three strips 1 ⅛ inch (3 cm) wide. D.

Orange fabric

Cut one strip 1½ inch (4 cm) wide. Cut into nine 1½ inch (4 cm) squares. E.
Cut two strips 1 inch (2.75 cm) wide. Cut into thirty-six 1 inch (2.75 cm) squares. C.

Block diagrams

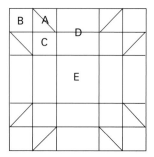 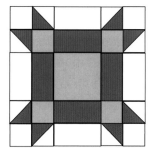

Construction

Refer to page 16.

Sew the three background and purple 1⅛ inch (3 cm) strips together. Press the seams open. Trim the strips so they measure ¾ inch (2 cm) from the seam line to the edge, and cut thirty-six 1½ x 1½ inch (4 x 4 cm) segments. See diagram 1.

Diagram 1

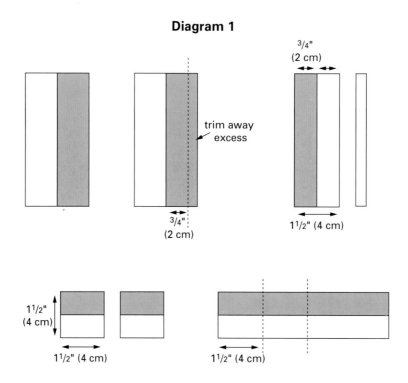

Layer the purple and background 1½ inch (4.5 cm) wide strips, right sides together. Cut into thirty-six 1½ inch (4.5 cm) squares. Cut in half diagonally once to yield seventy-two pairs of triangles. Sew together, press seams open and trim down into 1 inch (2.75 cm) bias squares.

Follow piecing diagram 2 to make thirty-six corner units. Press seams in the direction of the arrows.

Diagram 2 Corner unit assembly
make 36

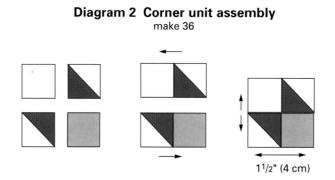

Lay out the pieces for one block as shown in diagram 3 and assemble a block. (If you are working in metric measurements, trim all seam allowances down to 0.5 cm.)

Assemble nine blocks. They will measure 3½ inches (9 cm) at this stage.

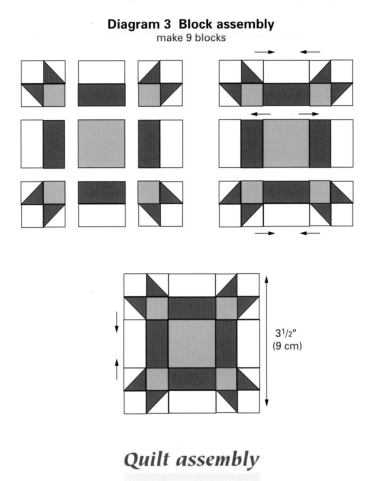

Diagram 3 Block assembly
make 9 blocks

Quilt assembly

Setting squares and triangles
From the remaining background section cut the following:
- Two 6½ inch (16.5 cm) squares. Cut diagonally twice. Side-setting triangles.
- Two 5 inch (13 cm) squares. Cut diagonally once. Corner triangles.
- Four 3½ inch (9 cm) squares. Setting squares.

Quilt top
Refer to page 30, and assembly diagram 4 below.

Lay out the blocks on the work area. Place the four 3½ inch (9 cm) setting squares in position.

Join the blocks, setting squares and side-setting triangles into rows. Press seams towards the setting squares and towards the side triangles. Join the rows together and press the seams open.

Refer to page 34 and square up the top, leaving ¼ inch (0.75 cm) seam allowances.

Diagram 4 Quilt assembly

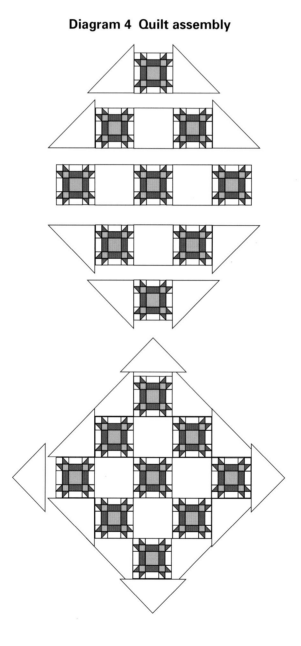

Borders

Refer to figures 25 and 26 on page 36–37.

Inner border Cut four 1 inch (2.75 cm) strips from the orange fabric.

Measure and attach the inner border strips. Trim the seam allowance of each strip after sewing down so the outer border seam allowance does not anchor it down. Trim the four inner border strips down to ⅝ inch (1.75 cm) wide.

Outer border Cut two strips 4¾ inches (12 cm) wide. Measure for the sides and cut a section this length from each strip. Attach to the sides of the quilt. Use the remaining strips for the top and bottom. Measure and attach.

Quilting

Refer to page 39.

Assemble the three layers. Pin baste in the centre of each block and in the inner border to begin with. Using a thread to match the background fabric, machine quilt in the ditch around each block.

Lightly free-motion quilt in the plain setting squares. This can be continuous if you take the stitching through the gap between the blocks. Do the same in the side and corner triangles.

Gently smooth the outer borders and pin alongside the inner border and the edges of the outer border. Change to a thread to match the outer border fabric and lightly free-motion quilt in the outer border, leaving a ½ inch (1.25 cm) area unquilted around the edges. The blocks should appear raised on the surface.

Neaten the edges of the quilt, leaving 4 inch (10.5 cm) wide borders.

Binding

Refer to figure 27 on page 40.

From the remaining border fabric cut two strips 1½ inch (4 cm) wide. Cut in half.

Measure and attach in the same manner as the borders, using a generous ¼ inch (0.75 cm) seam allowance.

Green and Gold

Quilt size 21¾ x 21¾ inches (55 x 55 cm)
Block size 2½ inches (6.25 cm)

This is a two-block quilt. There are a lot of different blocks that
can be combined to result in wonderful secondary designs.
This is a good example.

Requirements
Sewing machine and accessories
Rotary cutter, mat and rulers
Bias square ruler
Scissors, pins, quick unpicker and tape measure
Thread:
neutral colour for piecing
dark green for borders
to match background and green fabrics for quilting
Fabric, measurements based on 44 inches (112 cm) wide; amounts are
generous:
background: 20 inches (50 cm)
yellow: fat quarter
dark green: 10 inches (26 cm)
dark green: 14 inches (36 cm), for outer borders and binding
backing: 26 x 26 inches (66 x 66 cm)
Batting: 26 x 26 inches (66 x 66 cm)

Cutting

Dark green fabric

Cut one strip 1½ inch (4 cm) wide. From this cut thirty-six 1 x 1½ inch (2.75 x 4 cm) rectangles. A.

Cut a 6 inch (16 cm) wide strip. Cut this in half and put one piece aside for the bias strips. D.

From the remaining piece cut:

*   One strip 2 inches (5.5 cm) wide. H.
*   One strip 1 inch (2.75 cm) wide. From this cut four 1 inch (2.75 cm) squares. G. Put the remainder of the strip to one side for the sashing posts.

Block diagrams

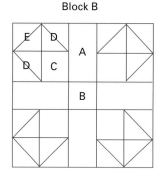

Yellow fabric

Cut two strips 1½ inch (4.5 cm) wide. E.

Cut one strip 1⅛ inch (3 cm) wide. F.

Cut one strip 1 inch (2.75 cm) wide. Cut into nine 1 inch (2.75 cm) squares. B.

Background fabric

Cut one 1½ inch (4.5 cm) wide strip. E. Cut in half to yield two strips.

Cut three strips 1 inch (2.75 cm) wide. Sashing strips.

Cut one strip 1 inch (2.75 cm) wide. Cut into thirty-six 1 inch (2.75 cm) squares. C.

Cut away a 6 inch (16 cm) strip. Cut this in half and put one piece aside for bias strips. D.

From the other half cut the following:

*   One strip 1⅛ inch (3 cm) wide. F.
*   One strip 2 inch (5.5 cm) wide. H.

From the remaining fabric cut two 6 inch (15.25 cm) and two 4½ inch (11.75 cm) squares. These are for the side and corner setting triangles. Put away for later.

Block assembly

Block A

Sew one yellow and one background 1¼ inch (3 cm) strip together. Press the seams open. Trim the strips so they measure ¾ inch (2 cm) from the seam to the edge. Refer to page 16 and cut into sixteen 1 x 1½ inch (2.75 x 4 cm) segments, as shown in diagram 1. F.

Diagram 1 Strip-pieced unit

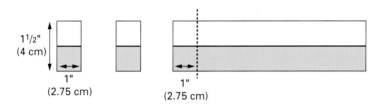

Layer the dark green and background 2 inch (5.5 cm) wide strips together. Refer to page 19.

Cut into eight 2 inch (5.5 cm) pairs of squares. Cut diagonally once to yield sixteen triangle pairs.

Sew the pairs together and press the seams open. Use the bias square ruler to trim these down to 1½ inch (4 cm) bias squares. H. Refer to page 20.

Follow the piecing diagram 2 and construct four blocks. (If you are working in metric measurements, trim the seam allowances down to 0.5 cm.) Press in the direction of the arrows.

Diagram 2 Block A piecing

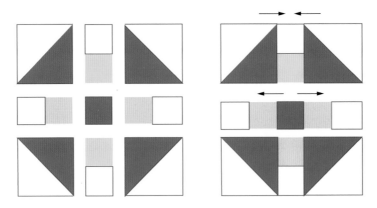

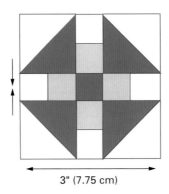

3" (7.75 cm)

Block B

Place the green and background 6 inch (16 cm) sections right sides together. Press. Refer to page 20. Cut nine bias strips 1⅛ inch (3.25 cm) wide.

Sew together along both long edges. Press. Using the 1 inch (2.75 cm) markings on the edge of the bias square, cut all the strip units into triangles. Open and press the seams open. Use the bias square to trim them down into seventy-two 1 inch (2.75 cm) squares. D. You should get eight triangles from each strip. If not, cut a few extra strips from the corner triangles.

Pair the two background 1½ inch (4.5 cm) strips with the two yellow ones, right sides together. Refer to page 19. Cut eighteen 1½ inch (4.5 cm) pairs of squares. Cut each pair diagonally once to yield thirty-six half-square triangle pairs. Sew these pairs together. Press seams open and trim down into thirty-six 1 inch (2.75 cm) bias squares.

Diagram 3 Assembling bias squares to form block unit
make 36

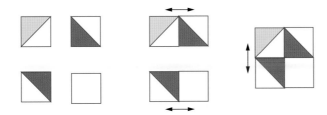

Follow the piecing diagram 4 and construct nine blocks. (If you are working in metric measurements, trim all seam allowances down to 0.5 cm.) The blocks will measure 3 inches (7.75 cm) at this stage.

Diagram 4 Block B piecing

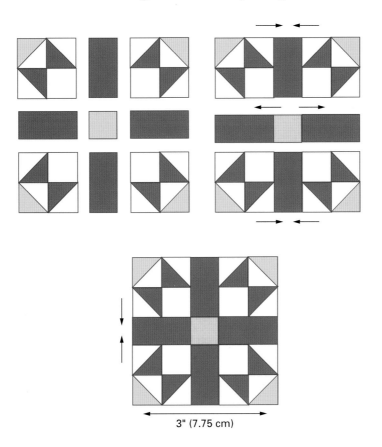

3" (7.75 cm)

Quilt assembly

Sashing strips

These are cut the exact width required.

From the pre-cut 1 inch (2.75 cm) strips cut the following:

- Twenty-six 1 x 3 inch (2.75 cm x 7.75 cm) strips.
- Ten 1 x 3½ inch (2.75 cm x 9 cm) strips.
- Cut twelve 1 inch (2.75 cm) squares from the leftover green 1 inch (2.75 cm) strip.

Assemble four sashing strip units as shown in diagram 4, using the 3½ inch strips at both ends of all units.

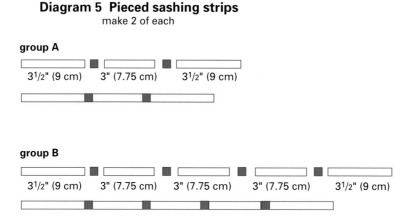

Diagram 5 Pieced sashing strips
make 2 of each

group A

3¹/₂" (9 cm)   3" (7.75 cm)   3¹/₂" (9 cm)

group B

3¹/₂" (9 cm)   3" (7.75 cm)   3" (7.75 cm)   3" (7.75 cm)   3¹/₂" (9 cm)

Quilt top

Lay out the blocks in order on the work area. Refer to quilt assembly diagram 6.

Refer to page 33. Press all seams towards the sashing strips, except the corner triangle seams. (If you are working in metric measurements, trim the seam allowances down to 0.5 cm.)

Sew a 3 inch (7.75 cm) sashing strip to the right-hand side of all blocks.

Sew a 3 inch (7.75 cm) sashing strip to the left-hand side of the first block in each row.

Join the blocks together to form the rows.

Sew a 3½ inch (9 cm) sashing strip to the top of row 1 and the bottom of row 5. Press.

Sew a group A sashing strip to the top of row 2 and the bottom of row 4. Press.

Sew a group B sashing strip to the top and the bottom of row 3. Press.

Diagram 6 Quilt assembly

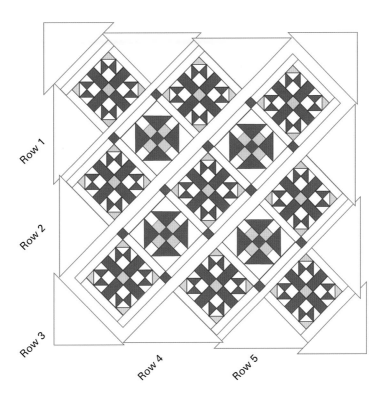

Position a half-square triangle at each end of rows 1, 2, 4 and 5. Make sure the long straight edges of the triangles are on the outside. Sew these in place. Press carefully as you are handling bias edges.

Join the rows together to form the top. The corner triangles are sewn in place last. Press the seams towards the triangles.

Borders

Refer to figures 25 and 26 on page 36–37.

Inner border Cut four 1⅛ inch (3 cm) strips from the yellow fabric. Measure and attach the side inner borders, then the top and bottom ones. Trim all four strips down to ⅝ inch (1.75 cm) wide, ⅜ inch (1 cm) wide when finished. (If you are working in metric measurements, trim the seam allowances down to 0.5 cm after each strip is sewn.)

Outer border From the green border fabric, cut two strips 4¾ inch (12 cm) wide. Measure for the sides and cut this amount from each strip. Sew to the sides. Using the rest of the border strips, measure and attach the top and bottom borders.

Quilting
Refer to figure 22 on page 33.

Assemble the three layers and pin baste. Quilt in the ditch around the blocks, then lightly quilt in the side-setting triangles. Quilt in the ditch around the inner border and then quilt a design of your choice in the outer borders, no wider than 3½ inches (9 cm).

Neaten the edges so the borders measure 4 inches (10 cm) wide.

Binding
Refer to figure 27 on page 41.

Cut two strips 1½ inch (4 cm) wide. Measure and attach the binding strips using a generous ¼ inch (0.75 cm) seam.

Cross and Crown

Quilt size approx. 15½ x 18½ inches (39.5 x 47 cm)

Block size 2½ inches (6.25 cm);

12 blocks square set 3 x 4 with sashing strips and posts

This quilt has a certain degree of difficulty, but with care in the handling

of the bias edges it will go together easily.

Requirements

Sewing machine and accessories

Rotary cutter, mat and rulers

Bias square ruler

Scissors, pins, quick unpicker and tape measure

Thread:

neutral colour for piecing

thread to match border fabric

quilting threads to match background and outer border fabrics

Fabric, measurements based on 44 inches (112 cm) width:

twelve assorted pink and purple fabrics: 6 x 12 inch (16 cm x 30 cm)

rectangle of each

background: 14 inches (40 cm)

inner border: fat quarter

outer border and binding: 14 inches (36 cm) in contrasting colour

backing: fat quarter

Batting: fat quarter

Cutting

Background fabric

Cut four strips 1 inch (2.75 cm) wide and cut the following (double the strips to make cutting easier):

- 48 squares 1 x 1 inch (2.75 x 2.75 cm) C.
- 48 rectangles 1 x 1½ inch (2.75 x 4 cm) B.

Cut a strip 6 inches (16 cm) wide and from it, referring to page 20, with the right side facing up, cut twelve bias strips 1½ inch (4 cm) wide. This must be cut in a single layer. D.

Put the remaining fabric to one side for the sashing strips.

Assorted fabrics

Refer to page 20.

From each of the twelve assorted fabrics, with the right side of the fabric facing down, cut one bias strip 1½ inch (4 cm) wide. Make the first cut through the top left-hand corner of the strip. D.

Up to four pieces can be layered and cut at the one time, but make sure that all pieces have right sides facing down.

From the two remaining triangles of each fabric cut four 2¼ inch (6.25 cm) squares, A, and one 1 inch (2.75 cm) square, E.

Block diagrams

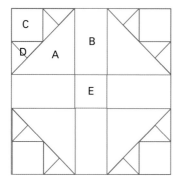
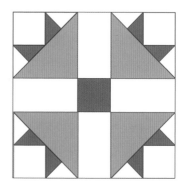

Construction

Bias squares

Refer to page 20.

With right sides together, to each of the background fabric bias strips sew one of the assorted fabric bias strips. Sew along both long edges. You will have twelve pairs of bias strip units.

Locate where the 1⅜ inch (3.75 cm) marks lie on the edges of the bias square. Line these up with the bottom stitching line, leaving ⅛ inch (0.5 cm) extending on the left-hand side. Cut along the right-hand side only of the bias square ruler to yield a triangle. Flip the bias strip unit over, line up the ruler and cut again. Make sure you leave the ⅛ inch (0.5 cm) on the left-hand side. You will need four triangles from each combination.

Remove any stitches from the points, press the seams open and trim down into 1⅜ inch (3.75 cm) bias squares.

Following diagram 1, and working with one fabric group at a time, cut each of the four bias squares in half diagonally to form mirror-image units. Cut with the seam facing you. Place one of the horizontal lines on the ruler over the seam line, and the edge of the ruler going diagonally through the corners. Gently push the cutter blade over the exposed seam to pre-cut it, then carefully cut from corner to corner. Keep together in their individual groups.

Diagram 1 Making mirror-image units

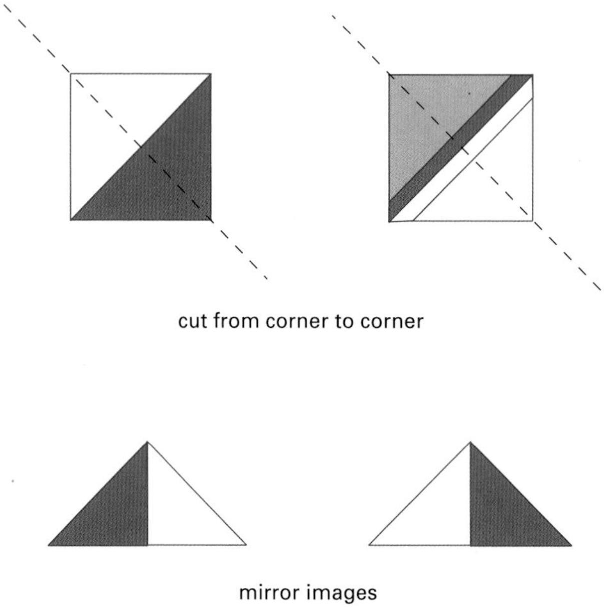

cut from corner to corner

mirror images

Refer to page 23. To form the triangle units, sew the mirror-image units to a 1 inch (2.75 cm) background square, as shown in diagram 2.

Diagram 2 Mirror-image units sewn to background square

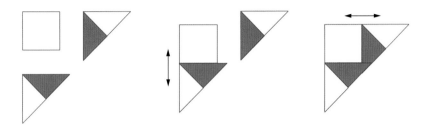

Repeat this process for all twelve assorted fabric mirror-image units. Press all seams open. Handle gently as the edges are on the bias.

Pair these triangle units up with the contrasting 2¼ inch (6.25 cm) squares. (If you are working in metric measurements, trim all following seam allowances down to 0.5 cm.)

To form the block, with right sides together, place a triangle unit over a contrasting 2¼ inch (6.25 cm) square (see diagram 3). Sew. Press the seams towards the contrast fabric.

Diagram 3 Assembling bias square triangle unit

Use the bias square ruler to trim the unit down to 1½ inch (4 cm) square. Trim away the excess from the square, as shown in diagram 4. Make four for each block.

Diagram 4 Trimmed bias square triangle unit

Follow the piecing order in diagram 5 to form the block. Match the centre square, E, with the small points or select at random. Press in the direction of the arrows. The last two seams are pressed open. Make twelve blocks. They will measure 3 inches (7.75 cm) at this stage.

Diagram 5 Assembling the block

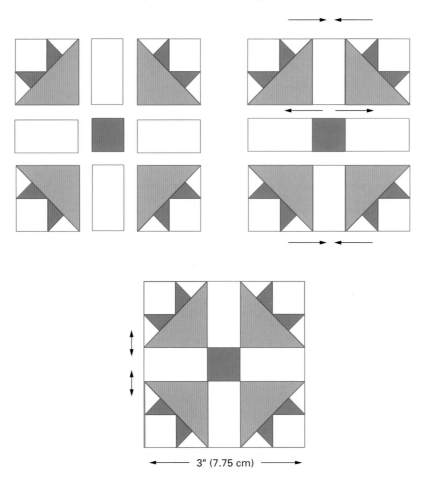

3" (7.75 cm)

Quilt assembly

Arrange the blocks into four rows of three.

Sashing strips and quilt top

From the leftover background fabric cut seventeen 1 x 3 inch (2.75 x 7.75 cm) strips. Sew one of these to the right-hand side of the first two blocks in each row, as shown in diagram 6. Press as sewn, finger-pressing gently towards the sashing strips. Join the blocks together to form four rows. Press. (If you are working in metric measurements, the seam allowances must all be trimmed down to 0.5 cm after pressing.)

Diagram 6 Joining plain sashing strips to the first two blocks in a row

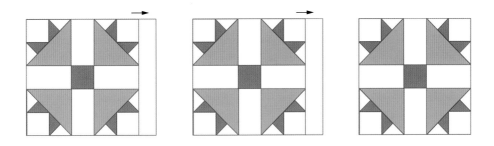

Cut six 1 inch (2.75 cm) squares from leftover pink and purple fabrics and, using the remaining nine 3 inch (7.75 cm) background strips, assemble the three horizontal sashing strips as shown in diagram 7. Press the seams towards the sashing, away from the squares.

Diagram 7 Assembling pieced sashing strips

Sew a pieced sashing strip to the bottom of the first three rows of blocks (diagram 8). Press towards the sashing strips. Sew the rows together to form the top, as in assembly diagram 9.

Diagram 8 Attaching the pieced sashing strips

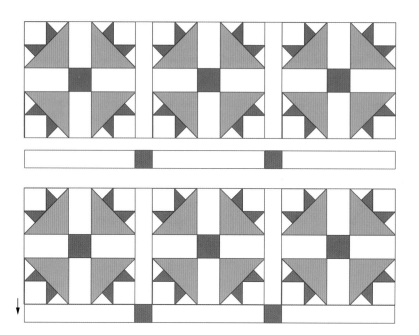

Borders
Refer to figures 25 and 26 on page 36–37.

Inner border Cut two strips 1 inch (2.75 cm) wide from the selected fabric. Measure, cut and sew. Remember to trim the seam allowances down after pressing each strip so they do not get caught up in the outer border seams. Trim the inner border strips down to ½ inch (1.5 cm) wide.

Outer border Cut two strips 4 inches (10 cm) wide from outer border fabric. Cut in half. Measure, cut and sew as for the inner borders. Give the top a good press.

Diagram 9 Quilt assembly

Quilting

Assemble the three layers and pin baste in each block and in the inner borders.

Quilt in the ditch around each block and in the inner and outer border seams. Pin baste the borders. Quilt a design of your choice in the outer border, no more than 3 inches (8 cm) wide so it doesn't get chopped off when squaring up for binding.

Square up the quilt, leaving the outer borders measuring 3¼ inches (8.5 cm) wide.

Binding

Refer to figure 27 on page 41.

From the remaining border fabric, cut two strips 1½ inch (4 cm) wide. Measure and cut one side and one top binding from each strip. Using a generous ¼ inch (0.75 cm) seam, sew the side bindings in place first, then the top and bottom bindings.

Grandmother's Lily Garden

Quilt size approx. 14½ x 19 inches (37 x 48 cm)
Block size 2½ inches (6.25 cm)

These delightful blocks are made using a variety of contrasting fabrics. The quilt is made up of eight blocks placed on point. The blocks appear to float, an illusion achieved by repeating the background fabric for the sashing strips and outer border.

Requirements

Sewing machine and accessories
Rotary cutter, mat and rulers
Bias square ruler
Scissors, pins, quick unpicker and tape measure
Ruler and black lead pencil
Embroidery needle
Thread:
  neutral colour for piecing
  to match background fabric for machine quilting
  green embroidery thread for stems
Fabric, measurements based on 44 inch (112 cm) width:
  background: 26 inches (66 cm)
  green: 12 inches (30 cm)
  lily fabrics: 6 x 8 inch (16 x 20 cm) rectangles of sixteen different fabrics sorted into eight contrasting pairs (e.g. bright and dark purple, medium and dark blue)
  backing: 18 x 23 inches (46 x 58 cm)
Batting: 18 x 23 inches (46 x 58 cm)

Cutting

Background fabric

Cut two strips 3 inches (7.5 cm) wide for the outer borders; put them away for later.

Cut two strips 1 inch (2.75 cm) wide; cut them into sixteen rectangles 1 x 1½ inch (2.75 x 4 cm). D.

Cut one strip 1⅛ inch (3 cm) wide. Put to one side for some of the sashing strips.

Open the remaining fabric out and place on the cutting mat, right side facing up. Refer to page 21. With the edge of the ruler going through the top left-hand corner and the 45° diagonal line on the left-hand selvedge, make a bias cut. Cutting across the bulk of the fabric, cut four bias strips 1½ inch (4 cm) wide (see diagram 1). B.

Block diagram

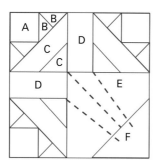 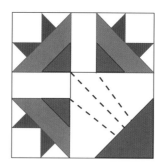

Diagram 1

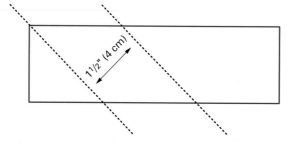

Cutting crosswise across the shortest width of the remaining fabric, cut one strip 2 inch (5.25 cm) wide. Cut into eight 2 inch (5.25 cm) squares. E.

Cut two 6 inch (15.25 cm) squares. Cut them diagonally twice to yield eight quarter-square triangles. Side-setting triangles. Pin together and put to one side.

Cut two 4½ inch (11.75 cm) squares. Cut them diagonally once to yield four half-square triangles. Corner triangles. Pin together and put to one side.

Cut twenty-four 1 inch (2.75 cm) squares from the leftover 1 inch (2.75 cm) strip and leftover corner triangle from the bias cut. A.

Put the remainder of the fabric to one side for the rest of the sashing strips.

Green fabric

Cut a 6 inch (16 cm) wide strip off the bulk of the fabric. Put the remaining fabric to one side for the inner borders and binding.

Place this strip onto the cutting mat, right side facing up. Cut eight bias strips 1½ inch (4 cm) wide. C.

Refer to page 17. Cut four 2 inch (6.25 cm) squares for the base of the block. F.

Print fabric combinations

Decide which fabrics will be the lily points and which ones will be the bases. There will be eight of each.

Lily point fabrics

Place the rectangles, right side facing down, on the cutting mat.

Cut one bias strip 1½ inch (4 cm) wide from all eight fabrics, referring again to diagram 1. B.

Lily base fabrics

Place the rectangles, right side facing up, and cut one bias strip 1 inch (2.75 cm) wide from each of the eight fabrics. C.

Construction

Unit A: lily points

With right sides together, sew two lily point 1½ inch (4 cm) bias strips to each of the four 1½ inch (4 cm) background bias strips.

Sew down one long side. Leave the needle in the fabric, lift the foot and slide another lily fabric strip into place on the remainder of the background strip, butting it up to the first one. Lower the foot and sew to the end. Sew down the other side. You will have a strip unit like diagram 2.

Repeat for the remaining strips to make four strip units like diagram 2. Cut apart to form eight bias strip units.

Diagram 2

Refer to page 22. Use the 1⅜ inch (3.75 cm) marks on the edges of the bias square to cut three 1⅜ inch (3.75 cm) triangles from each strip unit. Remove the stitches from the points of the triangles and press the seams open. Make sure you leave the ⅛ inch (0.5 cm) extending on the left-hand side of the bias square.

Trim these into 1⅜ inch (3.75 cm) bias squares.

Very carefully, cut all the bias squares in half diagonally once to yield mirror-image pairs of triangles (diagram 3a). Cut with the seam facing you. Place one of the horizontal lines on the ruler over the seam line, and the edge of the ruler going through the corners. Gently push the cutter blade over the exposed seam to pre-cut it, then carefully cut from corner to corner. Keep these mirror-image units together in their pairs (diagrams 3b, 3c).

Diagram 3 Cutting mirror-image lily points

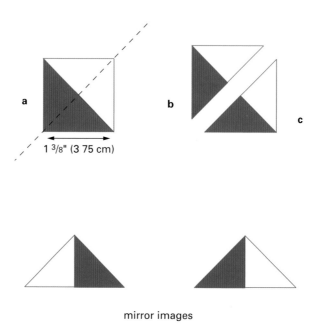

mirror images

Unit B: lily bases

To each of the eight 1½ inch (4 cm) green bias strips, sew a lily base 1 inch (2.75 cm) bias strip. Join along one long edge only. Offset the strips ¼ inch (0.75 cm) when lining up, as shown in diagram 4.

Diagram 4 Joining lily base elements

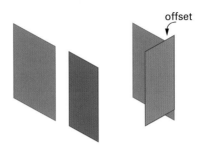

Press as sewn, then finger-press the seam towards the green fabric. (If you are working in metric measurements, trim the seam allowance down to 0.5 cm.) Press.

Use the rotary cutter and ruler to trim the lily base fabric strips down to ⅝ inch (1.5 cm) wide, from seam to outside edge, as shown in diagram 5. Do not trim the green strips. Have the ⅝ inch (1.5 cm) line on the ruler positioned on the seam allowance.

Diagram 5 Trimming lily base elements

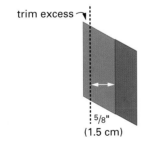

Block assembly

Sew two mirror-image lily point triangle units to each of the twenty-four 1 inch (2.75 cm) background squares as shown in diagram 6. Press the seams open. Handle gently as the edges will stretch.

Diagram 6 Lily point assembly

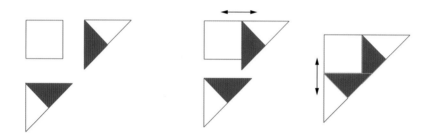

Match the lily point triangle units and contrasting lily bases together. Place the lily point sections on the combined green and lily base bias strip unit, as shown in diagram 7. The bias edges of the units are lined up with the edge of the lily base strips. Sew carefully. Use the quick unpicker to help keep raw edges together. Cut the sewn units apart where indicated by the dotted lines. Open out and press seams towards the base section. (If you are working in metric measurements, trim these seam allowances down to 0.5 cm.)

Diagram 7 Joining lily points units to lily base strip

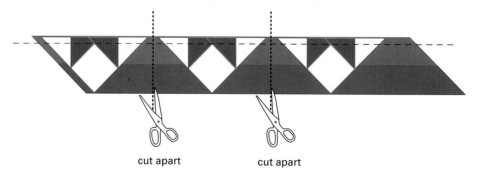

cut apart   cut apart

Use the bias square to trim the excess away from the base section, resulting in 1½ inch (4 cm) completed units, as in diagram 8.

Diagram 8 Completed lily block

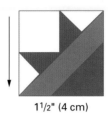

1¹/₂" (4 cm)

Stems

Using the lead pencil, lightly mark in the position of the stems on the right side of all eight of the 2 inch (5.25 cm) background squares. E. See diagram 9.

Diagram 9 Stem placement lines

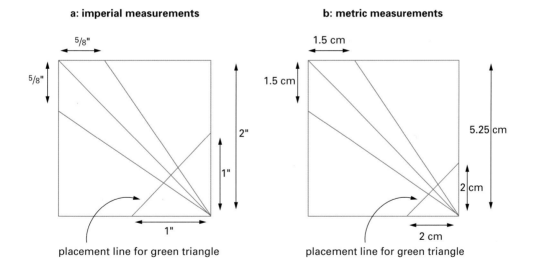

On the right side of each block, measure up 1 inch (2 cm) on both sides from the bottom right-hand corner of the background square. E. Make a dot and then rule a light line connecting them.

Cut the four green 2 inch (6.25 cm) squares, in half diagonally once to yield eight half-square triangles. F.

Line up a green triangle, bias edge to the line, centring the square over the triangle. Sew, using the edge of the green triangle as a guide. Press the triangle down. Trim away the excess background fabric from behind it. Use the rotary cutter and the bias square to trim away the excess from the green triangle, resulting in a 3 inch (7.75 cm) square. Using 2 strands of embroidery thread and stem stitch, embroider the stems. Don't make the stitches too tight as this will create distortion.

Lay out the pieces for one block. Following piecing diagram 10, construct the block. (If you are working in metric measurements, trim the seam allowances down to 0.5 cm after sewing.) Press seams in the direction of the arrows. Make eight blocks.

Diagram 10 Assembling the block

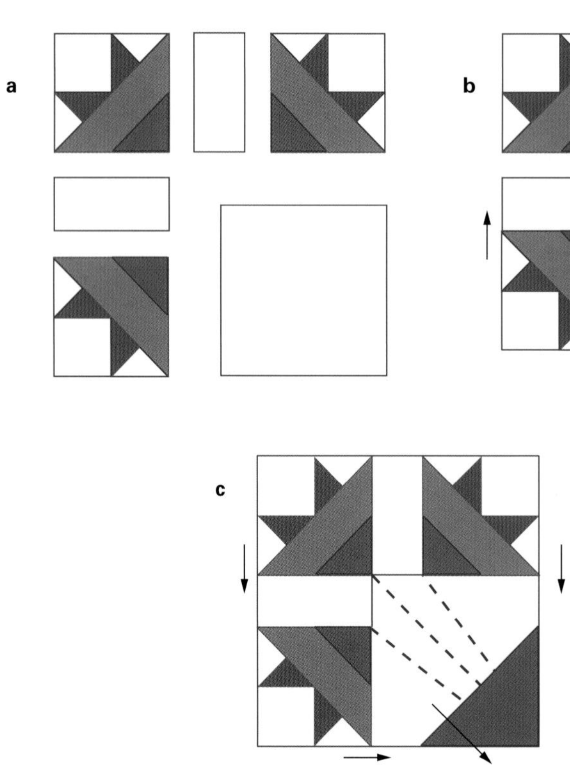

Quilt assembly

Sashing strips

These are cut too wide, and after sewing and pressing must be trimmed down to ¾ inch (2 cm) wide. They will be ½ inch (1.25 cm) finished width after the top is assembled. Refer to page 17. (If you are working in metric measurements, trim all seam allowances down to 0.5 cm.)

From the pre-cut 1⅛ inch (3 cm) wide strip cut the following:

- One strip 16½ inches (40 cm) long. This is cut too long, the excess being trimmed after the quilt top is assembled.
- Two strips 10 inches (25.5 cm) long.

From the remainder of the background fabric cut the following:

- Twelve strips 1⅛ x 3 inches (3 x 7.75 cm).
- Two strips 1⅛ x 4 inches (3 x 10.25 cm).

Press all seams towards the sashing strips.

Quilt top

Arrange the blocks in order beside your machine and refer to the four assembly diagrams (diagram 11).

Sew a 3 inch (7.75 cm) sashing strip to the right-hand side of each blocks, and then to the left-hand side of the first block in each row (diagram 11a). Press and trim.

Sew a 4 inch (10.25 cm) strip to the top of row 1 and bottom of row 4 (diagram 11a). Press and trim.

Join the blocks in rows 2 and 3 (diagram 11a). Press and trim.

Sew a 10 inch (25.5 cm) strip to the top of row 2 and bottom of row 3. Trim down and mark sashing strip matching points on both these strips (diagram 11a).

Place the side-setting triangles in position as shown and sew in place (diagram 11b).

Join rows 1 and 2 together to form the top half of the quilt. Join rows 3 and 4 together to form the bottom half (diagram 11c).

Sew the 16½ inch (40 cm) strip to the bottom of combined rows 1 and 2 (diagram 11c). Press and trim. Mark the matching points for the short sashing strips and join the two halves together, matching the marks to form the quilt top. Sew the corner triangles in place (diagram 11d).

Neaten the edges of the quilt, leaving a ¼ inch (0.75 cm) seam allowance on all four sides.

Diagram 11 Quilt assembly

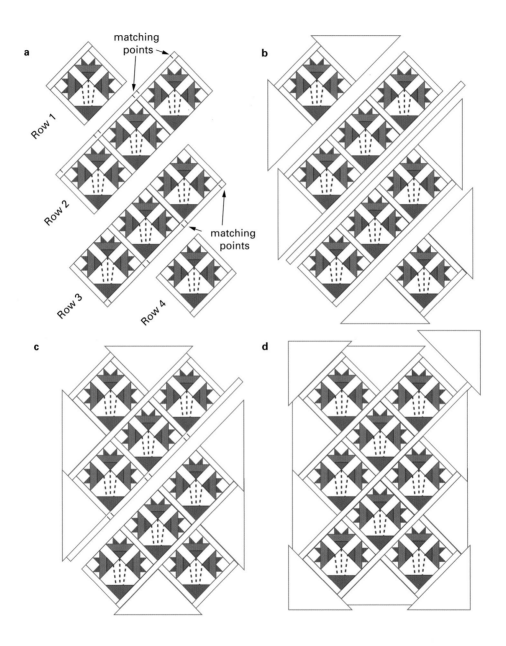

Borders

Refer to figures 25 and 26 on 36–37.

Inner border Cut two strips 1 inch (2.5 cm) wide from the green fabric.

Measure and attach the inner borders, doing the sides first, then the top and bottom. Press seams towards the borders. Trim the seam allowances of each strip down to ⅛ inch (0.25 cm) after pressing. This stops the next row of stitching from anchoring them. Trim all four borders down to ½ inch (1.5 cm) wide. They will be ¼ inch (0.75 cm) wide after the outer borders have been attached.

Outer border Using the two pre-cut 3 inch (7.5 cm) wide strips, measure and attach as for the inner borders, doing the sides first, then the top and bottom. Press seams towards the outer borders.

Quilting

Assemble the three layers. Quilt in the ditch around each block. Do some free-motion quilting in the outer border and in the side and corner setting triangles. Avoid quilting in the sashing strips and inner borders.

Neaten the edges of the quilt, leaving the borders 2½ inches (6.50 cm) wide.

Binding

Refer to figure 27 on page 41.

Cut 2 strips 1¼ inch (4 cm) wide from the green fabric.

Measure and attach the bindings using a ¼ inch (0.75 cm) seam.

Forest Pansies

Quilt size approx. 24 x 24 inches (61 x 61 cm)
Block size 3 inches (7.5 cm); 13 blocks set on point with sashing strips

This is a very striking little quilt that is easier to piece than it looks. There are a lot of pieces but the end product is worth the effort.

Requirements

Sewing machine and accessories
Rotary cutter, mat and rulers
Bias square ruler
Scissors, pins, quick unpicker and tape measure
Thread:
  neutral colour for piecing
  dark green for attaching sashing strips and borders
  machine quilting threads to match background fabric and borders
Fabric, measurements based on 44 inch (112 cm) width; amounts are generous:
  background: 12 inches (30 cm)
  dark green: 36 inches (1 m) for piecing, sashing strips, borders and bindings
  rust: 12 inches (30 cm) for piecing, sashing posts and inner borders
  orange: 4 inches (10 cm) for piecing
  backing: 27½ inches (70 cm) square
Batting: 27½ inches (70 cm) square

Cutting

Background fabric

Cut two 1½ inch (4.5 cm) strips. A.

Cut three 1¾ inch (4.5 cm) strips. Cut into fifty-two 1¾ inch (4.5 cm) squares. Cut diagonally once to yield 104 half-square triangles. B.

Cut two 1 inch (2.75 cm) strips. Cut into fifty-two 1 inch (2.75 cm) squares. C.

Rust fabric

Cut two 1½ inch (4.5 cm) strips. A.

Cut one 1½ inch (4 cm) strip. Cut into thirteen 1½ inch (4 cm) squares. F.

Cut one 1 inch (2.75 cm) strip. Sashing posts.

Cut two 1¼ inch (3.25 cm) strips. Inner border.

Dark green fabric

Cut three strips 5 inches (12.75 cm) wide. Outer borders.

Cut four strips 1½ inch (4 cm) wide. Binding.

Cut two 1 inch (2.75 cm) strips. Cut into fifty-two 1 inch (2.75 cm) squares. E.

Cut two 6½ inch (16.5 cm) squares. Cut these diagonally twice to yield eight quarter-square triangles for the side-setting triangles.

Cut two 5 inch (13 cm) squares. Cut these diagonally once to yield four half-square triangles for the corners.

The remaining fabric is for the sashing strips.

Orange fabric

Cut two 1½ inch (4 cm) strips. D.

Block diagrams

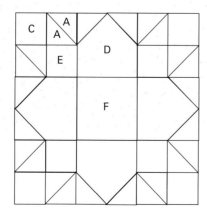 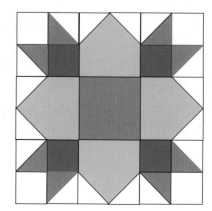

Construction

As there are a lot of pieces involved, it is easier to keep things under control if you assemble enough units for three or four blocks at one time and construct the blocks, then repeat the process.

Unit A

Diagram 1 Unit A templates

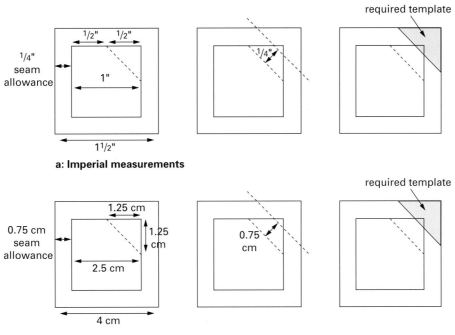

a: Imperial measurements

b: Metric measurements

I found I had to resort to separate imperial and metric templates for unit A to make the instructions easier to follow (diagram 1). On a piece of strong paper, draw the required shape the finished size—1 inch (2.75 cm) square. Add a ¼ inch (0.75 cm) seam allowance to all four sides. As the actual stitching/seam line intersects two sides of the finished square at ½ inch (1.25 cm), draw a line connecting these two points. Now add a ¼ inch (0.75 cm) seam allowance outside this line. It must be parallel. The resulting triangle is the shape required for the template which you will use to remove two corner sections from the squares.

Cut out the template and lightly tape it to the back of the bias square ruler with the long edge of the triangle level with one edge of the ruler, as indicated in diagram 2. Make sure you select the correct measurement, inches or centimetres.

Diagram 2

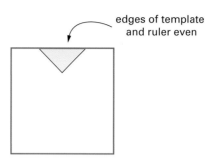

edges of template
and ruler even

Layer the two orange strips together, right side to wrong side. Cut twenty-six pairs of 1½ inch (4 cm) squares. After cutting one pair, slide the strip away and place the template over the bottom left-hand corner of the pair. Have the short edges of the template in line with the sides of the squares and carefully cut along the edge of the ruler (diagram 3a).

Turn the trimmed squares over and repeat for the other corner (diagram 3b).

Put to one side. Cut another pair and repeat. You will need fifty-two trimmed units (twenty-six pairs).

Diagram 3 Trimming corners of the square

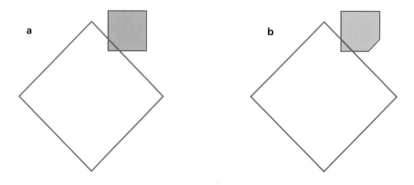

Following diagram 4, sew two of the 1¾ inch (4.5 cm) background half-square triangles to the base of each of the trimmed 1½ inch (4 cm) orange squares. These triangles are too big. Carefully centre the cut edges of the square over the triangles. Excess is trimmed after both triangles have been sewn and pressed. These units can be chain-pieced (there are fifty-two of them) but

I suggest that you do one first as a trial. Use the edge of the trimmed square as a sewing guide. Press the seam to the triangle. (If you are working in metric measurements, trim the seam allowances down to 0.5 cm.) Trim each unit into 1½ inch (4 cm) squares.

Diagram 4 Assembling unit A
make 52

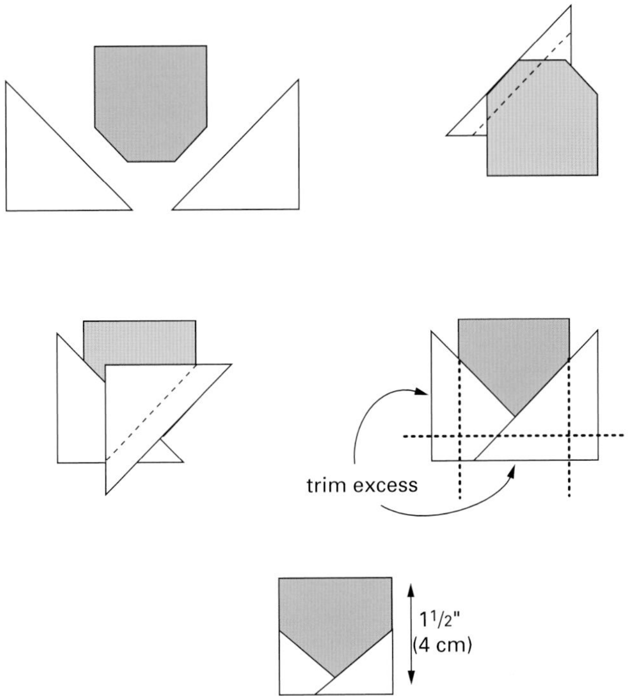

trim excess

1½"
(4 cm)

Unit B

Refer to page 20.

Layer two 1½ inch (4.5 cm) background strips and two rust 1½ inch (4.5 cm) strips, right sides together, to form two strip pairs. Cut fifty-two pairs of 1½ inch (4.5 cm) squares. Cut diagonally once to yield 104 pairs of half-square triangles.

Sew the triangle pairs together. Press the seams open. Use the bias square ruler to trim these down into 1 inch (2.75 cm) bias squares.

Diagram 5 Assembling unit B
make 52

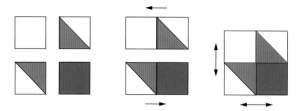

Following diagram 5, assemble fifty-two of unit B. Press seams towards the dark green and background squares.

Block assembly

Diagram 6 Block assembly

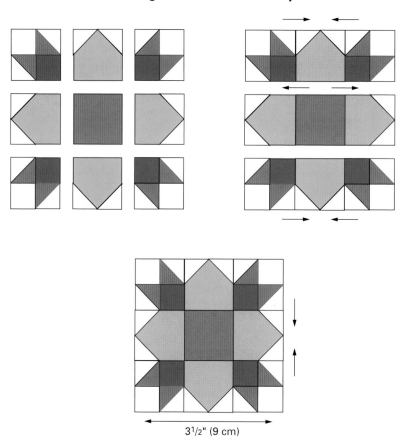

3¹/2" (9 cm)

Lay out the pieces for one block and assemble, following the piecing order given in diagram 6. (If you are working in metric measurements, trim the seam allowances down to 0.5 cm after joining each section together.)

Make thirteen blocks.

Quilt assembly

Sashing strips and posts

Cut one 3½ inch (9 cm) wide strip from the remaining dark green and cut thirty-six 1 x 3½ inch (2.75 x 9 cm) strips.

Cut twenty-four 1 inch (2.75 cm) squares from the 1 inch (2.75 cm) wide rust strip.

Following diagram 7, assemble two each of sashing strip groups A, B and C. (If you are working in metric measurements, in this case there is no need to trim seam allowances.) Press seams towards the strips.

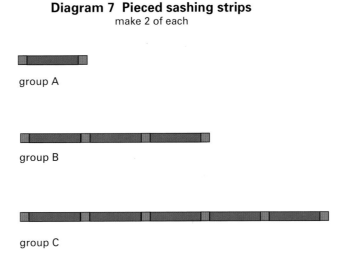

Diagram 7 Pieced sashing strips
make 2 of each

group A

group B

group C

Diagram 8 Quilt assembly

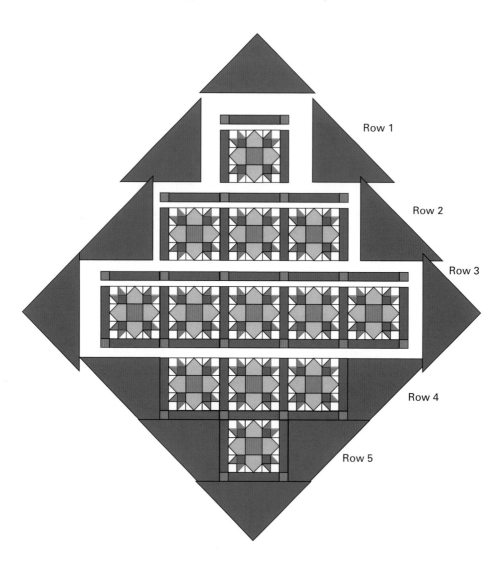

Row 1

Row 2

Row 3

Row 4

Row 5

Quilt top

Change to the dark green thread.

Lay out all the blocks beside your machine. Refer to page 33 and the quilt assembly diagram 8.

Sew a plain sashing strip to the right-hand side of each block.

Sew a plain sashing strip to the left-hand side of the first block in each row. Press.

Join the blocks together to form the rows.

Sew a group A sashing strip to the top of row 1 and the bottom of row 5. Press lightly. Press all seams towards the sashing strips. (If you are working in metric measurements, trim the seam allowances down to 0.5 cm.)

Sew a group B sashing strip to the top of row 2 and the bottom of row 4. Press lightly.

Sew a group C sashing strip to both sides of row 3. Press lightly.

Place the rows in order on the work area. Lay the green side-setting triangles in place at the ends of rows 1, 2, 4 and 5. Sew these in place. Press towards the sashing strips, away from the triangles.

Join rows 1 and 2 together and rows 4 and 5 to form two sections. Sew row 3 to the bottom of the top section. Press. Sew the bottom section in place.

Attach the corner triangles and press the seams towards them.

Press the quilt top so it is lying nice and flat.

Neaten the edges of the quilt, leaving a ¼ inch (0.75 cm) seam allowance extending on all four sides.

Borders

Refer to figures 25 and 26 on page 36–37.

Inner border Cut the two 1¼ inch (3.25 cm) wide rust strips in half.

Measure and attach the sides first, then the top and bottom. Trim the seam allowances down to ⅛ inch (0.5 cm) wide after sewing each strip in place. Press seams towards the borders.

Trim these four inner border strips so they are ½ inch (1.5 cm) wide.

Outer border Cut one of the 5 inch (12.5 cm) wide strips in half. These are for the sides of the quilt; the other two long strips are for the top and bottom. Measure and attach. Give the top a good press.

Quilting

Assemble the three layers together. Refer to page 39.

Pin baste in the centre of each block, in the inner border and then the outer border.

Using a thread to match the background fabric, machine quilt in the ditch around each block.

Change to dark green thread and lightly free-motion quilt in the side and corner triangles. You can do all edges in the one go if you carefully machine in the gaps where the sashing posts touch the inner borders.

Gently smooth the outer borders and pin alongside the inner border and

CREATIVE MINIATURE QUILTS

then about ¼ inch (0.75 cm) in from the edges. Lightly free-motion quilt in the outer border, leaving a ½ inch (1.25 cm) area unquilted around the edges. Neaten the edges of the quilt, leaving 4¼ inch (11 cm) wide borders.

Binding

Refer to figure 27 on page 41. Use the four pre-cut dark green 1½ inch (4 cm) wide strips.

Measure and sew the bindings in place, using a generous ¼ inch (0.75 cm) seam.